DATE DUE

Demco, Inc. 38-293

NEW MEXICO IN THE
NINETEENTH CENTURY:
A PICTORIAL HISTORY

NEW MEXICO

In the Nineteenth Century

A

PICTORIAL
HISTORY

By Andrew K. Gregg

—

UNIVERSITY OF NEW MEXICO PRESS · ALBUQUERQUE

Endpapers: Front—"Freighting salt in New Mexico," drawn by Dan Smith (*Frank Leslie's Newspaper*, Nov. 28, 1891). Back—Cowboys betting on a fight between bulls, drawn by W. A. Rogers (*Harper's Weekly*, Nov. 22, 1880).

© The University of New Mexico Press 1968. All rights reserved. Manufactured in the United States of America by the University of New Mexico Printing Plant, Albuquerque, New Mexico 87106. Library of Congress Catalog Card No. 68-56225 First edition.

PREFACE

The Nineteenth Century in New Mexico began with the discovery of copper in a wild corner of a remote Spanish territory and ended with the construction of a new capitol for a territory ready to become one of the United States.

The copper mine at Santa Rita is still in operation. In 1900, although New Mexico had been a territory for over fifty years, it had to wait another twelve to become a state.

Tumultuous times, tremendous growth, economic upheavals, and revolts were all a part of Nineteenth Century New Mexico, yet the rest of the world knew relatively little of what had happened.

In a sense, the image of New Mexico has been distorted by the public interest in its three best-known citizens—Billy the Kid, Kit Carson, and Geronimo. These three captured the stage before the eyes of the world. The rough image they formed continued in countless books, magazine articles, movies, and television shows to shape a picture that the state of New Mexico is still trying both to live down and capitalize on.

Many Nineteenth Century travelers, reporters, and artists wrote and drew what the East expected. They showed a New Mexico full of colorful or savage Indians, cowboys, outlaws, sun-scorched deserts, and sharp mountains.

Sandwiched between the blood and the thunder were archeological reports, ethnological studies, railroad surveys, paeans to the Santa Fe trade, autobiographies, and immigration invitations.

Until the middle 1880s, the rest of the world knew almost nothing about New Mexico. There had been a few obscure books, reports, and autobiographies published. They are well known to historians now, but to the rest of the world from the 1600s until the arrival of the first traders from the East, New Mexico was an unknown land. Charles III, king of Spain, knew so little about his distant territory that in 1775 he asked the Viceroy of Mexico if there were some native New Mexico pelicans available for the royal zoo. (There weren't.)

In 1821, New Mexico and Mexico separated from Spain. In the confusion and opportunistic politicking that followed, violence was a natural outcome. The Pueblo Indians revolted in 1837. When Governor Albino Perez tried to defeat them in battle outside Santa Fe, they lopped off his head and stuck it atop a pole in the capital plaza. A rich ex-sheepherder, who may have started the rebellion, took over the government and put down the revolt.

The East knew nothing of this; Mexico cared little.

At the beginning of the War with Mexico, Kearny's army captured Santa Fe, fought a battle at Brazito, and put down a rebellion at Taos.

The gold fields of California and the Halls of Montezuma got the headlines.

When the Civil War loomed, the South prepared to invade the new territory, then march on to capture the gold in California to finance the Confederate government. Gen. Henry H. Sibley and his army moved north to victory at Valverde, defeat at Glorieta, and then straggled back to Texas in a disastrous rout.

The East worried about the battles of Ft. Donelson, Pea Ridge, and Shiloh.

The Apaches, at first friends of the newcomers from the East, turned against them to become the "human tigers," the Huns of the Southwest.

But now the East and Europe had begun to learn about New Mexico. While the hostiles ravaged isolated areas, settlers poured into the new territory. They were spurred by the hopes of fertile land, new markets, new jobs.

An 1869 guidebook to the West and South warned settlers against the Indians of New Mexico. "The fiendish Apache roams at will over the vast arid plains and among the lonely gorges of a large portion of the territory, ever on the watch for booty and blood."

The postmaster at Santa Fe, however, had a more encouraging view. "In the vicinity of Santa Fe . . . land is very good and can be had at low prices. The climate is healthful, and the seasons mild and delightful. Labor commands from $1 to $5, according to skill." Actually, average agricultural wages in New Mexico at that time were $25 per month without board.

Placid New Mexico boomed. The newcomers brought railroads, oysters, smelters, land grant swindles, longhorns, sorghum, full length mirrors, tuberculosis, and a host of other benefits and plagues.

The boom had been in the making for thirty years.

One of the first to write about New Mexico was Lt. Zebulon Pike. He was sent to the Southwest, probably on a spying mission, in 1806. The following February, Pike and his troops were captured by Spanish soldiers in Colorado and taken to Santa Fe. He got the first guided tour of the area, from there to Chihuahua. There he was held prisoner. He was later released and his pessimistic report, published in 1810, advised that New Mexico be left to the Indians. But his report showed that trade with the area was feasible.

The first traders arrived and found business profitable, if a bit risky. Their stories helped make the Santa Fe Trail a byword in commerce.

A few years later, the East read about the capture of Texas filibusterers in the early 1840s. About 300 had been captured and taken to Mexico. About half survived starvation and disease and were released in 1842. Public indignation, plus the reports of the traders, stirred interest in the acquisition of New Mexico. Then came the Mexican War and Kearny.

With Kearny came the first of many artists to visit New Mexico. John Mix Stanley had come overland with a trading caravan to Santa Fe and found a berth as an army artist. He sketched his way to California and returned to the East where he found fame as a painter of Indians.

Heinrich Balduin Mollhausen, a German, immigrated to the United States in 1849. He toured the Rockies with Prince Paul of Wurttemberg in 1851. The expedition was forced out by Indians, but Mollhausen stayed behind in Nebraska at a lonely river fork when a passing stagecoach, packed full, had to leave him behind. He was snowbound there for two months, gnawed frozen wolf meat, and was almost ambushed by Pawnees. He killed two before he was rescued by friendly Indians. He moved on to Missouri, but the West drew him back. He came to New Mexico as an artist for the Whipple expedition in 1853. He returned in 1857 with Ives' expedition to the Colorado River. Then he went back to Berlin to show his paintings and write hair-raising novels of frontier life.

With the railroads and stagecoaches came magazine artists like W. M. Cary, Theodore Davis, Frederic Remington, and the team of Paul Frenzeny and Jules Tavernier.

The first artists to stay in New Mexico for any length of time came in the 1880s. Charles Craig sketched in Taos in the summer of 1881. The godfather of the Taos Art Colony, Joseph H. Sharp, visited Santa Fe in 1883 and painted at Taos in 1893. He met Bert Phillips and Ernest Blumenschein later in Europe, talked with them and told them of the beauties of the Southwestern scenery—Taos' in particular. Blumenschein visited Taos in 1898 and, later that year, he and Phillips decided to make a wagon trip from Denver to Mexico. They got as far as Taos and stayed.

Men like these helped form the world's image of New Mexico. There were others, too. Unnamed and unknown artists—hacks—labored away to depict the blood and thunder that appeared in the cheaper magazines and dime novels of the day. Some of them knew little about the West and its scenery or customs. A few copied earlier pictures and added embellishments or changed the scenery to fit new plots. They also helped form an image, and their version has proved a strong one. While hundreds saw Stanley's scenes of New Mexico mountains and deserts, thousands saw Remington's dramatic pictures of the chase after Geronimo. Millions are familiar with the simple sketches of Billy the Kid killing his guards at Lincoln and his death at the hands of Pat Garrett.

All these pictures made up the image—the face that the raw territory of New Mexico presented to the world. This is the way the world saw us.

The pictures used in this book are the works of human hands and talent. Some are reproduced from stone lithographs. Others are woodcuts from paintings or drawings. Some are reproductions of woodcuts from photographs. This is not a photo book—there are no halftone pictures of photographs. This is the way the world saw New Mexico in its own time, and with the hand craftsmanship that characterized that time.

For instance, in some of the pictures from *Harper's Weekly* faint white lines may be seen. The *Harper's* engravers, to save time, had a system that called for expert talent and care that has not been seen since. After the original picture was sketched on a large block, it was sawed into squares and passed out to the engravers. As many as thirty-six of them worked on their own blocks. The pieces had to match into one large picture when they finished. The squares were bolted together and a wax mold of the engraving was made. Electrotyping was used to make the final engraving used in the printing.

The halftone screen and photographic reproduction meant the end for the hand engravers. Their days of careful carving and squinting through magnifying glasses were gone.

Because of the time envolved in making a good engraving, and the consequent expense for skilled labor, publishers often borrowed, perhaps stole, woodcuts and other engravings. Some views have been used many times. Sometimes engravers sketched a copy of a picture on a block of wood and cut out all the parts that would appear white. They added their own talent in the process.

The picture source given for a particular scene in this book does not mean that it is the only place where that picture was used.

In general, the old artists and engravers showed a pretty good idea of what New Mexico was like.

Kit Carson was important. He helped open the West. The novels about his life inspired many young men to go west.

Geronimo was important in his time. His depredations helped many a frontier community survive on Army payrolls. (The money spent in fighting Apaches could have bought every warrior a nice plot of land in the Southwest. Yet, in 1877, congress wouldn't be bothered with appropriating funds to pay the army that was serving on the frontier.)

Billy the Kid is probably New Mexico's single top tourist attraction.

But in the days when people remembered and believed in manifest destiny, when a new world was waiting—a world that promised wealth or escape—young men turned toward the West. The Great West! Ho, for the Great West!

Where in the Great West? Well, some place where there is good land, good wages for day laborers, a place where a shrewd trader could make some money. Some wanted to fight Indians, others to forget their name in the states; the lure of the open range and clear sky drew young men.

But they came.

ANDREW K. GREGG
November 22, 1968

CONTENTS

(*Land of Sunshine*, July, 1898.)

CONQUISTADORES

THE FIRST Europeans to visit New Mexico were Alvar Nuñez Cabeza de Vaca and three other men. They had been shipwrecked on the coast of Florida. De Vaca led them across Texas, through (some authorities say near) New Mexico and into Mexico.

One of them, Estevan the Moor, returned as a guide for Fray Marcos de Niza in 1539. Estevan went on ahead as they neared Hawikuh pueblo, near Zuni. The natives killed him, reportedly in outrage when Estevan made advances to their women. When Fray Marcos learned of this, he trudged back to Mexico.

Next came Coronado's expedition. It reached Zuni on July 7, 1540. Where Fray Marcos had predicted cities filled with riches, the soldiers found a mud town with hundreds of armed Indians lining the rooftops.

When the Indians showed no signs of surrendering, the Spaniards attacked. Their first assault was met with a barrage of arrows and stones that drove them back. But steel swords and armor were stronger than rocks and arrows. The Indians surrendered in less than an hour.

Sketch of a buffalo (American bison), was drawn by one of Oñate's men, 1599. (Winsor.)

Snarling, curly bison of 1558 has little relation to original animal. (Winsor.)

This early Spanish version looks like a feathered draft horse. (*Land of Sunshine*, July, 1898.)

SEVEN GOLDEN CITIES

WHEN CORONADO arrived in 1540, New Mexico was thought to be a land of riches, of mines of gold, silver, and even quicksilver. And why not? Anything was possible in the New World. Only 20 years before Cortez had plundered Mexico of millions in gold, silver, and jewels.

Seven years earlier, an illegitimate ex-swineherd named Francisco Pizarro had captured the Inca of Peru, accepted a ransom of a room full of gold and then murdered him.

Surely there must be something worthwile in this land of snowy mountains and burning deserts that stretched invitingly north of Mexico.

The story of the Seven Cities of Cibola had begun years before in Europe. The seven cities legend had been shifted from the Antilles to Brazil, to China, and now was placed north of Mexico.

The legend of the treasures of Gran Quivira began as a tale told by an Indian slave at Pecos to lead Coronado's expedition off to starve on the Staked Plains. Coronado reached Quivira in central Kansas, found only a collection of mud huts and promptly executed the slave. He also found that the legend of the seven cities had no basis in fact.

In short, New Mexico as a land of riches was a failure.

The explorers marched back to Mexico, but they had found that land and water were available. The next wave was of colonists. The first try, in 1590, was an aborted one. The leader, Gaspar Castaño de Sosa, did not have authority to colonize.

Don Juan de Oñate did. His army of soldiers and settlers left Mexico in 1598, traveled to San Juan Pueblo and started the first capital of New Mexico.

The colonists had found their land and New Mexico quickly stepped into the modernity of the 17th century.

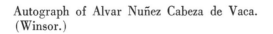

Autograph of Alvar Nuñez Cabeza de Vaca. (Winsor.)

Signature of Francisco Vasquez de Coronado. (Winsor.)

THE MODERNITY of the 17th
century included peonage,
slavery, the Inquisition, and
disease. Life was crude and
cruel, but missions, towns, and
small haciendas slowly spread
up and down the rivers. Some of
these sites are almost forgotton
today—places like Cañada,
Galisteo, Armijo, and Senecu.

In 1680 a Pecos firebrand,
Po-pe, led a successful revolt
that was the culmination of
years of resentment against the
Spaniards.

In one sweeping slash, the
Indians surrounded and besieged
Santa Fe. Outlying settlers and
missionaries were killed.

The Spaniards trapped inside
the town held out for eleven
days. On August 21, they
surged out to attack the Indians.
They killed about 300 and took
47 captives. The next day the
settlers and soldiers, totalling
about a thousand, moved out of
the capital and began a long and
deadly journey to Mexico.

With the Spaniards gone, the
Indians fought each other. Po-pe
was murdered.

The Spaniards returned in
1692. Don Diego de Vargas and
his soldiers took the capital
peacefully and raised the banner
of Spain again.

Settlers returned the next year
to reoccupy Santa Fe, Cañada,
and some of the other towns.

Exploration and contacts with
the rest of the Southwest began
in the 18th century. Trails went
out from Santa Fe to the Pacific
coast, to western Mexico, and to
Texas and Louisiana. By 1792,
when Pedro Vial made the first
trip to St. Louis, New Mexico
was ready for trade with the rest
of the country.

First modern horses probably were brought to New Mexico by Coronado in 1540.
(*Century*, Jan., 1889.)

Romantic view of de Vaca crossing the Southwest. Actually, the
four Spaniards wore deerskins.
(*Harper's*, July, 1880.)

Today a super-highway speeds traffic through Apache Pass, once the scene of Indian ambushes on the Arizona-New Mexico border. (Cozzens, 1876.)

Mouth of Night Creek, a tributary of the Gila, is explored by Emory's party. (Emory, 1848.)

SHIPROCK is a spectacular red volcanic neck near Farmington. Rising 1,450 feet above the desert, it reminded early explorers of a sailing ship.

It was an active volcano in the Cenozoic Era some 25 million years ago.

According to Navajo legend, Shiprock is a "rock with wings" that carried their people to these lands from across great seas.

Several dikes extend from the base of the rock. A large one stretches about three miles to the south.

Monument Rock (top) in Santa Fe Canyon in the Sangre de Cristos. (Ritch, 1885.)

Shiprock (center) was never, in historical times, surrounded by lakes as shown in this fanciful sketch. (Thayer, 1888.)

Abiquiu Peak (bottom) near Espanola. This and the Shiprock picture were redrawn from Macomb's work. (Thayer, 1888.)

THE ABIQUIU area is one of the most interesting in the state, with unusual geological features, many fossils, and the nearby Ghost Ranch.

The town of Abiquiu was built some time before 1747 on the site of an old Tewa pueblo. In 1779 the village had 851 inhabitants. Most of them were Indian slaves. The Indian population slowly dwindled while the Spanish population grew. By the time the early Army explorers arrived, the village was almost entirely Spanish with some mixtures of Indian blood.

Fra Cristobal Mountains marked the northern end of the Jornada del Muerto. (Davis, 1857.)

THE Jornada del Muerto, or Journey of the Dead Man, began where travelers left the Rio Grande and skirted the east side of the Fra Cristobal Range. They moved south for about ninety miles to rejoin the river near Mt. Robledo. The trip generally took about six days and there was little or no water along the route.

The railroad now follows the old Jornada del Muerto through old cattle towns like Engle and Cutter and past the old Spanish campgrounds.

The City of Rocks between Deming and Silver City is now a state park. (Bartlett, 1854.)

THE City of Rocks, seen above, is now a state park with running water, a campground and a cactus garden.

The twisted, pitted rocks are of sugarlump welded rhyolite tuff that show millions of years of erosion by wind and water. The rock was formed from small particles of hot lava spewed from the mouth of an ancient volcano. The frothy mass ran over the ground in a thick layer, hardened into a light and porous mass and was covered with ash. The ash dissolved into the tuff and softened it for wind and water to do the carving job seen today.

The Burro Mountains, southwest of Silver City. (Bartlett, 1854.)

Sandstone formations (above) in the Chaco Canyon area appear to be modern buildings and turreted castles. This drawing, from Cozzens, is a copy of a painting made by one of the Kern brothers for Lt. Simpson. Both illustrations are gross exaggerations. (Cozzens, 1876.)

When John R. Bartlett's men surveyed southwestern New Mexico they were captivated by the strange wild country. Here they approach Mule Creek. (Bartlett, 1854.)

The Mogollon mountains (below), rich in minerals, beautiful, and deadly. Gold was discovered here in 1875. Its discoverer, Sgt. James Cooney, was killed by Apaches and is buried in a vault of rock near the town of Mogollon. (Sitgreaves, 1854.)

Lt. Emory's expedition in 1846 moves along the valley of the Mimbres River in south-western New Mexico. (Emory, 1848.)

Indian pictographs were seen by Emory near Red Rock on Gila River. (Emory, 1848.)

Stein's Peak and Stein's Pass near the New Mexico-Arizona border. The pass, along the Butterfield stage route, was a favorite spot for robbers. (Cozzens, 1876.)

Headwaters of the Gila River in the Mogollon Mountains. (Cozzens, 1876.)

A mirage seen on the plateau west of the Rio Grande near Hillsboro. (Cozzens, 1876.)

Volcanic trap dike at Pope's Well, south of Santa Fe. A trap dike is a dense sheet of vertical volcanic rock jutting up to form a ridge. (Newberry, 1876.)

Pinos Altos Mountains near the Santa Rita copper mines
were an Apache stronghold for many years. (Dunn, 1886.)

(Below) heading east on one of the first expeditions into
the Navajo country, an artist on the Simpson expedition
sketched the mountains rising behind Jemez pueblo. (Simpson, 1852.)

View of the Rio Grande below Rincon. (*Harper's*, April, 1886.)

TRAVELERS in New Mexico were often at the mercy of strange elements.

Dust devils that approached tornado force, and occasional tornados, were problems.

Mirages were frequently seen. The most popular story is that of the lake or stream ahead that turns out to be a mirage. However, cities and mountains have also been seen.

Fierce blizzards were apt to roar out of the north. They still are, but the weather bureau is able to give enough warning so that tourists and ranchers are relatively protected.

Wind and dust storms are common, especially in the spring. Early travelers, when caught in a sand storm, holed up as best they could and made themselves as small and tight a target as possible.

Waterholes and springs dried up during droughts. Travelers and even experienced scouts might make a dry march for days to find no water where they had expected some. Indians had various ways of getting water from cactus, carrying it in the intestines of a slaughtered animal or simply carrying a pebble in the mouth to stimulate saliva. Inexperienced white men just died of thirst.

Not a factory smokestack, but a prairie tornado. (*Harper's*, April, 1854.)

"False ponds," mirages as seen by James A. Brewerton in the 1840s. (*Harper's*, April, 1854.)

Cabezon Peak, near the Rio Puerco, stands in a valley that was once Albuquerque's breadbasket. Drought and agricultural over-use turned the valley into a desert. The town of Cabezon, once thriving, is now a ghost town and closed to the public. (Macomb, 1876.)

This exaggerated drawing of a yucca plant shows it to be about forty feet high. The yucca is the state flower of New Mexico. (Drake, 1887.)

Cabezon, sticking into the air like a thick thumb, is the core of an ancient volcano. It is a landmark and was a target for stage coach travelers from Santa Fe to Fort Wingate. (Simpson, 1852.)

THE ORGAN Mountains, because of their distinctive fluted shape, are one of the most spectacular ranges in New Mexico.

They overlooked a section of the Camino Real, where supplies slowly moved north to the capital in Santa Fe and the missions of New Mexico. Later came Baylor's "Buffalo Hunters" to capture Mesilla at the beginning of the Civil War. Next came Sibley's Army of New Mexico. A few months later the remains of his shattered army trudged along the same trail on their dreary retreat south after their defeat at Glorieta.

This view of the Organs does not show the distinctive fluting of the rock formations. (*Harper's*, April, 1885.)

The Organ Mountains and the Rio Grande, near Las Cruces. (Cozzens, 1876.)

Organ Mountains, redrawn with addition of a boat (in the desert!). (Bartlett, 1854.)

THE LUSH Mesilla Valley, west of the Organs, was settled early in the 19th century. Mesilla was originally just south of New Mexico Territory after it became part of the United States and the town was settled by Mexicans who didn't want to be part of the U.S.

The valley, along with its prosperous farms and vineyards, became part of Mexico through the Gadsden Purchase.

Mesilla was the capital of the Confederate Territory of Arizona for awhile. Its high point of political turbulence came late in the 19th century, when Democrats and Republicans had rallies on the same day. The two rallies collided on the square in a battle of fists and revolvers that left several dead.

Washington Pass, through the Chuska Mountains of the Navajo country in northwestern New Mexico, was a favorite route of explorers. (Simpson, 1852.)

Mount Taylor, near Grants, is an ancient sacred mountain for the Indians. Lava flows form a *malpais* around much of its base. (Simpson, 1852.)

Some of New Mexico's magnificent mesas inspired sketches such as this. Note the "pueblo ruins" on top of the rocks on the right. (Newberry, 1876.)

Another exaggerated view, this time of the City of Rock near Deming. (Cozzens, 1876.)

N.ORR-CO.N.Y

Palisades of the Staked Plains in eastern New Mexico. The undulating, grassy plains are bordered by these bluffs near Tucumcari. The plains may have been named for the stake-like bluffs, for the towering yucca stalks growing there, or from stakes driven in the ground to indicate nearby water. (Whipple, 1853-4.)

Lieutenant Emory's troops leave their wagons at the Rio Grande near the base of Fra Cristobal Mountains in 1846. The expedition continued on foot and horseback across western New Mexico and on to San Diego. (Emory, 1848.)

Hot springs near Silver City were well known in the area. A health resort was later established here. (Bell, 1870.)

ONE BIG attraction in New Mexico is the variety of its geologic features. Hot springs and other signs of volcanic activity abound. These include Shiprock, Capulin, the Valle Grande, malpais lava flows, Soda Dam, and others.

New Mexico mountains are volcanic, like Capulin; fault block, like the Sandias, or complex. Nearly every geologic feature, including sea action and continental glaciers, has left some sort of mark in the state.

In the Paleozoic era, northern New Mexico was a shallow island in a sea teeming with long squids and other denizens of salt water.

Continental glaciation brought wet weather and mammoths, camels, and other Pleistocene mammals to New Mexico. Their bones are found in many parts of the state.

In some of the higher areas, Alpine glaciation gouged holes in the mountains and filled tremendous lakes like the one in the Estancia Valley, which stretched from Moriarty to the White Sands.

Scenes of unusual geological formations, some of them very exaggerated, appeared in many early accounts of travel in New Mexico.

"Canon Infierno" is probably Hell's Canyon, a rugged gash that connected Isleta Pueblo with the Manzano mountain towns of Chilili and Escobosa. (Howe, 1852.)

Waterfall on the Rio Bonito. (Ritch, 1885.)

TRAVELERS between Santa Fe and Taos had a rough time in the 1840s.

James Brewerton heard "the sudden report of an escopeta fired by some unseen hand . . . which coupled with the sharp whiz of a ball within anything but a pleasant proximity of my right ear."

Brewerton returned the greetings with a load of buckshot and galloped off to safety.

The road between Santa Fe and Taos as James Brewerton saw it in 1848. (*Harper's*, April, 1854.)

Another scene on the road to Taos. The crosses mark the graves of travelers killed by bandits. (*Harper's*, April, 1854.)

The placer mountains near Golden—the Ortiz and the San Pedros. Gold was mined here many years before the discovery of gold in California. (Simpson, 1850.)

El Morro (Inscription Rock) is now a national monument.
The oldest legible signature is that of Don Juan de Oñate in
1605. (Thayer, 1888.)

The base of El Morro rock is covered with names carved
into the soft stone. Among the many "paso por aqui" en-
tries is that of De Vargas, 1692 shown here as sketched
by an artist on the Simpson expedition. (Simpson, 1852.)

Atop El Morro rock are the ruins of an earlier pueblo, still visible to the tourist who climbs the landmark that is now a national monument. (Whipple, 1856.)

Loaded burros shown here are probably being prepared for a trading trip from Zuni. (*Harper's Weekly*, Jan. 28, 1882.)

BANDELIER
CLIFF DWELLINGS

THE ANASAZI (Navajo for "ancient ones"), were the basketmakers who lived in the cliffs. Their towns thrived by A.D. 500. Droughts in the late 1200 s forced them out of their cliff homes to find dependable water supplies. They became the Pueblo Indians living along the rivers today.

A restoration of the Tyuonyi ruins at Bandelier National Monument. Indians lived until A.D. 1550 in this unusual circular primitive apartment house built of tuff. (Thayer, 1888)

The stone pumas carved in lava were sacred hunting shrines of the Cochiti. They are about five miles from the Rito de los Frijoles on the Potrero de las Vacas. (*Scribner's*, Jan., 1893)

The cliff ruins at Bandelier National Monument. Many other cliff dwellings are scattered around the Pajarito Plateau near Los Alamos. (*Harper's Weekly*, Sept. 7, 1889)

CHACO CANYON

THE great ruins in the Chaco Canyon of
northwestern New Mexico were thriving pueblos
in fertile grasslands in A.D. 1100. They were
abandoned in the 1200s. Hungo Pavi, like Pueblo
Bonito, was a large D-shaped complex of rooms.

Hungo Pavi Pueblo, redrawn from the original sketch in
Simpson's *Report*. (Thayer, 1888.)

Pueblo Pintado, one of the rela-
tively unknown pueblo ruins in the
Chaco Canyon area. (*Harper's*,
Aug., 1882.)

The pueblo of Hungo Pavi (below) as Lt. J. H. Simpson thought it
would have looked in its prime. (Simpson, 1850.)

Ruins of the church at Pecos in the 1840s. It was here that the legend of the Gran Quivira began when an Indian slave was told to lead Coronado's expedition into the desert to die. (Simpson, 1852.)

Pecos Mission. Army explorer Lt. Abert was told that a huge serpent in the kiva there needed a yearly sacrifice of a virgin. The site is now a national monument. (Abert, 1847.)

OLD MISSIONS

MANY missions were founded in the
early 1600s. Most were deserted after
the Pueblo Revolt of 1680. Two of
them, Gran Quivira and Pecos, are
national monuments. Abó, Jémez, and
Quarai, along with the ruins of those
pueblos, are state monuments. The
ruin of Kuaua Pueblo is Coronado
State Monument. Other pueblos ruins
that are national monuments are Aztec,
Bandelier, Chaco Canyon, and the Gila
Cliff Dwellings.

Women getting water from the Rio
Grande. (*Harper's*, April, 1885.)

Ruin of Abo mission, founded in 1629
and abandoned about 1670. It is now a
state monument. (Abert, 1847.)

Ruins of Pecos, re-sketched. (Drake, 1887)

USING one early illustration, later artists redrew pictures for use in books and magazines. The two large pictures on the opposite page were done by John Mix Stanley, artist with Kearny's expedition, and published in Emory's *Notes on a Reconnoissance* in 1848. The changes made in the three small pictures on this page are not enough to disguise their obvious sources in Stanley's work.

(*Harper's*, April, 1854)

An Indian foot race. (*Harper's*, May, 1885)

(*Harper's*, April, 1854)

Ruins of the mission at Pecos Pueblo (above). The mission was started in 1617. The pueblo was abandoned in 1838, when only seventeen survivors of disease and hostile Indian attacks were left. (Emory, 1848)

"Ruins of the Aztek Church" (below). Because of their massive structures and their legend of Montezuma, the Pueblo Indians were first thought to be related to the Aztecs of Mexico. (Emory, 1848)

Quarai mission, established in 1629. It was a village of the Tewas. They abandoned it in 1674 and moved to the El Paso area. (*Scribner's*, April, 1893.)

"THE CITIES that Died of Fear" have become a tourism trademark in New Mexico. The missions and pueblos at Gran Quivira, Quarai, Abo, Tenabo, Tajique, Chilili, and possibly Manzano and Torreon were abandoned a few years before the Pueblo Revolt of 1680 because of drought, disease and harrassment by the Apaches. Some of the towns were later reoccupied. The string of pueblos are generally called the Salines, because of their nearness to the salt lakes near Mountainair.

Gran Quivira. Not the one sought by Coronado in 1541, but a village known as "Las Humanas." (*Scribner's*, April, 1893.)

Ruins of the mission at Quarai. "On the Rhine it would be a superlative," said Lummis, "in the wilderness of the Manzanos it is a miracle." (*Scribner's*, April, 1893.)

The watch for Montezuma, drawn by the artistic team of Paul Frenzeny and Jules Tavernier. (*Harper's Weekly*, May 22, 1875.)

PUEBLO INDIANS

MOST OF THE PUEBLOS of the 19th century are still occupied and look much as they did a hundred years ago. But there are some changes. More of the Indians are leaving the pueblos for work in the towns. Schooling is accepted as a part of modern life. Highways have brought tourists to the pueblos to visit and buy both authentic craft goods and cheap gimcracks.

The Pueblo Indians were always willing to integrate or cooperate with the outside world —on their own terms.

The Indians of Acoma and Laguna went to court to solve a problem that would have been settled with arrows and guns if it had been a case of Pueblo against Navajo. The lawsuit involved a painting of St. Joseph that had been brought to Acoma in 1629 and installed in the new mission. It was borrowed by the people of Laguna for help during a drought. It was returned to Acoma, then stolen and taken back to Laguna. The Acomans sued. The case dragged on for five years until the Supreme Court awarded the painting to Acoma in 1857.

The Pueblos continued to be independent or to accept the white man's ways when it suited them.

Taos Indians refused to let meddling whites into their kivas after rumors of immoral practices had been thrown about. The Indians said that when they were admitted to Masonic rites, they might think about letting the whites visit the kivas. In the meantime, there were shotguns to enforce their privacy.

In 1917, Santo Domingo Indians captured state troopers who were looking for rustlers and held them until the Indian agent arranged for their release.

In 1965, Isleta leaders handcuffed and evicted the priest at their pueblo.

All this does not necessarily indicate that the Pueblo Indians are warlike or hostile. They are warm, friendly people who welcome visitors who will respect Indian customs. They have, in fact, put up with many intrusions of privacy, meddling, and intensive anthropological studies that would enrage the average middle-class Anglo. (Would you accept several hundred curious strangers on your front lawn and in your living room while your family had Christmas dinner and opened the presents under the tree?)

There are 18 Indian Pueblos in New Mexico. Some, like Zuni, Taos, and Acoma, are well known and have many visitors. Smaller ones, like Sandia and Santa Ana, are overlooked by the tourists. All the Pueblos welcome visitors, but some are more conservative and have tighter restrictions on pictures, dress, and the areas where the tourists may visit.

Northern section of Taos pueblo. (Davis, 1857.)

(Sweetser, 1891.)

Two other views of Taos pueblo are shown in an 1891 guide to the United States. The picture on the right shows the extensive fields at the pueblo.

(Sweetser, 1891.)

Taos Creek divides the Pueblo into two sections. (Thayer, 1888.)

THE FIRST artists who came to New Mexico lived at Taos and made the pueblo famous. Bert Phillips and Ernest Blumenschein came to New Mexico in 1898. Their wagon broke down near Taos. Blumenschein, taking a broken wheel into the town for repairs, was so struck by the beauty of the area that the two decided to stay. This was the beginning of the Taos art colony, which used the symbol of a broken wagon wheel.

This exaggerated view of Taos pueblo resembles a Babylonian ziggurat. (Peters, 1874.)

The northern part of Taos pueblo as it appeared in 1882. (*Harper's*, Aug., 1882.)

The distinctive features of Taos: doorless walls, ladders and ovens. (Tenney, 1880.)

Indian failing in hunting is chastised by his wife. (Beadle, 1878.)

San Geronimo de Taos, inhabited for more than 600 years, is one of the best known Indian pueblos in New Mexico. (Davis, 1857.)

Indians pressing grapes (below). Traditionally, they did not use wine themselves. Priests had vineyards and wineries and sometimes used Indian labor. (*Harper's Young People*, Dec. 30, 1890.)

The hair style, boots and blanket of the pueblo women are shown here. (Wood, 1894.)

A pack train leaving Taos. Annual trading fairs at the pueblo began in prehistoric times. (Brooks, 1887.)

The Green Corn Dance, held in Taos on the 25th and 26th of July. It is also held at several other New Mexico pueblos. (Cozzens, 1876.)

San Juan Pueblo, near Española, was visited by Oñate in 1598. He set up the first capital of New Mexico nearby. It lasted for more than ten years before it was moved to Santa Fe. (Ritch, 1882-83.)

Room in Taos Pueblo. This clearly shows roof construction in large rooms. Where the vigas are not long enough to span the whole room, pillars and a pole support shorter vigas in the center. (U.S. Geo. & Geo. Survey, 1881.)

Kearny's army passing San Felipe. This painting was done by John Mix Stanley. (Emory, 1848.)

The mission at San Felipe Pueblo, shown near the center, was built about 1700. (Abert, 1847.)

The Corn Dance at Santo Domingo is one of the Southwest's most magnificent spectacles. This is the clown dancer. (U.S. Census, 1890.)

Female dancer in the Corn Dance at Santo Domingo. The *tablita* or tablet used as her headdress gave rise to the name Tablita Dance, often used to designate the ceremony. (U.S. Census, 1890.)

Male dancer in the Corn Dance at Santo Domingo Pueblo. The feathers, fox tail, gourd, and other accessories are not capricious decorations but have precise traditional meaning. (U.S. Census, 1890.)

The Pueblo of Laguna. The lake for which it was named dried up centuries before this fanciful drawing was made. (Thayer, 1888)

The fields at Laguna are shown in this more realistic sketch by an artist who probably worked from a photograph. (*Harper's*, Feb., 1891)

The church of San Jose de Laguna was built in 1699. (*Harper's*, Feb., 1891.)

Houses and carretas at the Pueblo of Laguna. (*Harper's*, Feb. 1891.)

The pueblo of Acoma, near Laguna, sits atop this high mesa. (Abert, 1847.)

IN THE old days, every piece of wood, bit of dirt, and drink of water for Acoma was carried up the steep and narrow path. Before 1629, the only path up was a ladder-like string of finger- and toe-holes gouged out of the rock.

The rugged isolation of Acoma Pueblo shows in this drawing. (Drake, 1887.)

This steep and narrow trail (right) up the mesa was the best path to Acoma for hundreds of years. (Abert, 1847.)

Another early sketch of the famous Sky City pueblo. (Tenney, 1880.)

OF THE many churches built in the earliest days, only one or two are still in use. One is San Miguel in Santa Fe. The other, San Esteban Rey at Acoma, may be the original one built in 1629.

This church at Santa Clara was built about 1692 and lasted until 1909. (*Harper's Weekly*, Sept. 7, 1889.)

Feast day at the old Acoma church. Acoma has its annual fiesta on Sept. 1. (*Scribner's*, Dec., 1891.)

Not far from Acoma, the Enchanted Mesa rises precipitously 430 feet above the plain. A few hardy men have scaled its height and found a few artifacts but no traces of dwellings. (U.S. Census, 1890.)

The town of San Miguel del Vado was an important stop for traders along the Santa Fe Trail. Members of Kendall's Sana Fe expedition of 1841 were imprisoned here before being sent to Mexico City. (Abert, 1847.)

SINCE the 1840s, when U.S. Army expeditions first visited them, the Pueblo Indians have been subjected to many anthropological studies. Old Spanish records and archaeological excavations have helped fill in their histories.

A quiet corner in the pueblo of Santo Domingo. (Roberts, 1885.)

Two Zia sisters, judged to be the best pottery artists of their pueblo. (BAE 11th Annual Report.)

Indian rock carvings are found in all parts of New Mexico. The two examples shown above have a curious history: they were copied in the sketchbooks of expedition artist Richard H. Kern "by some members of the band of Taos Utahs, who killed the old guides, Williams and Dr. Kern, in the spring of 1849." (Schoolcraft, 1856.)

A French artist produced this drawing of a Jemez Pueblo warrior, from a sketch by Abbe Domenech made on his travels. (Domenech, 1862.)

THE INDIANS at Santo Domingo took part in the Pueblo Revolt of 1680. The inhabitants of nearby San Felipe joined with those at Santo Domingo to kill the priests and soldiers at the latter pueblo. In 1837, they allied with other Indians in a revolt, caught Gov. Albino Perez just outside Santa Fe and lopped off his head.

Santo Domingo Pueblo is noted for its jewelry. Its people had lived in several other locations, including Galisteo Creek and the Jemez Mountains. (Ladd, 1891.)

This early view of Santo Domingo apparently was drawn from a written description. (Abert, 1847.)

WITH the coming of the railroad in 1879, tourists poured into the Territory. Visits to Indian pueblos were highlights of their trips. Some stayed for longer periods and brought back large collections of Indian goods. Many of the finest specimens of Navajo blankets, Zuni dolls and other items are now seen in Eastern museums.

Dancers at the Indian pueblos were willing to pose for artists and photographers in the 1800s. (*Harper's Weekly*, Sept. 7, 1889.)

The pueblo of Tesuque is ten miles north of Santa Fe. Each year the pueblo honors its patron saint, San Diego, with ceremonies on November 12th. (Ritch, 1882-83.)

Tesuque Pueblo in the 1880s. The first village, abandoned during the Pueblo Revolt, was about three miles east of the present one. (*Harper's Weekly*, Sept. 7, 1889.)

The saddle cradle is still used in many pueblos. Drawing from a photo by Charles Lummis. (*Harper's Young People,* Jan. 20, 1891.)

Early sketches of Indian warriors such as the one at left were drawn with a classic treatment that made them resemble Greek soldiers. (Domenech, 1862.)

After the coming of the Spaniards, the pueblos adopted the wooden wheeled carreta, oxen, and pack burro. (Ladd, 1891.)

Santa Ana Pueblo, near Bernalillo. Its people first built a pueblo on Black Mesa near San Felipe but moved to their present site in 1692. (Abert, 1847.)

Pueblo Indians such as these, said one 19th century visitor, are "the only native race whose presence on the soil is not a curse to the country." (Bell, 1870)

"Sun, Silence and Adobe," the primitive peace of the Pueblo Indians as eulogized by Charles Lummis. (*Scribner's*, Dec., 1891)

Model of Zuni Pueblo was built at the National Museum in Washington and shown there. (*Century*, Jan., 1885.)

ZUNI PUEBLO

ZUNI is probably the best known Indian pueblo in the United States, despite its conservatism, isolation, and the relatively small amount of publicity it has received compared to Acoma and Taos.

Millions of college students become acquainted with Zuni life and customs through "Patterns of Culture," a book by Ruth Benedict that is used in many anthropology courses.

Studies of Zuni began in the middle of the 19th century when the early Army explorers visited the pueblo and found it almost completely lacking in contact with the white man. Even the Spanish people were viewed with distrust and barred from seeing any of the Indian dances there.

One of the first men to seriously study the Zunis was Frank Cushing, who lived with them from 1879 to 1884. The Zunis distrusted him at first, but gradually adopted him. He eventually became a priest of one of their societies. Articles by or about him appeared in contemporary magazines. His books on Zuni are still republished.

The purity and authenticity of Zuni rituals has attracted anthropologists ever since Cushing's time. They find the Zunis friendly and hospitable, but reticent in explaining old complicated rituals.

Zuni burial was simple and quick. The interment was held outside the pueblo. (*Century*, May, 1882.)

Zuni as shown in one of the earliest New Mexico travel articles. (*Harper's*, Sept., 1858.)

Group of shy Zunis (left) pose for an early magazine artist. (*Popular Science*, September, 1874.)

Zuni war party. Warriors who had taken scalps could belong to the Bow Society. (*Century*, May, 1883.)

Frank Cushing in Zuni costume. He was initiated into the Bow Society. (*Century*, August, 1883.)

Water is poured on clown dancers before annual trip to sacred lake. (*Jnl. of Am. Eth.*, 1891.)

Zuni maiden carrying water. (*Harper's*, August, 1875.)

DANCES play an important part in the life of the Zunis. They invoke rain, increase fertility, and bring success in war.

Ceremonial games, contests, races, and gambling also are designed to promote the welfare of the pueblo by asking the gods for help.

Priests who perform the rites have received long and arduous training in the intricate steps and prayers they must perform. Moreover, they must prepare themselves by remaining benevolent and continent for several days and undergoing ceremonial washing, taking purgatives, and fasting. Any variance or neglect of these rituals may bring failure to the ceremony, disapproval from the gods, and droughts.

Priests begin their training in childhood and slowly work their way up in their societies until they are ready for their high offices.

Zuni buffalo dancer. (Sitgreaves, 1854.)

Zunis planting corn use traditional sharpened sticks. (*Century*, May, 1883.)

Shalako ceremony is Zuni's best known and most magnificent one. Held each December, it lasts all night. (*Century*, February, 1883.)

Part of Shalako rite is performed in a new home being blessed by the ceremony. (*Century*, February, 1883.)

Street scene in Zuni as a *Harper's* artist sketched it. (*Harper's Weekly*, January 28, 1882.)

Buffalo Dance at Zuni as seen by members of the Sitgreaves expedition in the summer of 1853. The soldiers spent several months there while waiting for Navajo troubles to subside. (Sitgreaves, 1854.)

Zunis mining turquoise at a
sacred spot in the mountains.
(*Century*, February, 1883.)

SORCERY among the Zunis was a capital
crime. The magician might have cast an
evil spell over some person or he might
simply be a scapegoat in a time of trouble.

Cushing tells of one sorcerer, called
"the Bat," (seen on the right), who
hung for more than five hours before he
confessed that he had kept the rain
from falling. He promised to bring rain
within four days.

"Four days passed," wrote Cushing,
"and no rain came; nor did the 'Bat' do
as he had promised, for he returned home
only to threaten revenge on the
priesthood, and since the fifth day no
one outside of that priesthood has ever
seen a trace of the 'Bat'."

Most sorcerers reformed after torture,
said Cushing, but they would be executed
if their victims died or if it was believed
that they caused natural troubles such
as drought or sandstorms.

Sorcerer is tortured by being hanged by
the wrists. (*Century*, May, 1883.)

Around the council fire, where much of the serious business of governing the Indian pueblos takes place. (*Harper's*, June, 1882)

View of Zuni shows prominent stake corrals. (Schoolcraft, 1856.)

Modern (1875) Zuni pottery and shards of old pots. (*Harper's*, Aug., 1875.)

Pa-lo-wah-ti-wa, governor of Zuni pueblo in 1883. Colored headbands were standard wear for all Zuni men. (*Century*, Feb., 1883.)

Zuni street scene. Flat stone on the right is used for making paper bread. (*Century*, Dec., 1882.)

Men and women working or sunning themselves on the terraces of Zuni in the summer. (*Century*, Dec., 1882.)

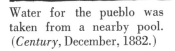

Zuni, (below), its fields and, in inset, a pack train of wood loaded on burros. (*Century*, December, 1882.)

Water for the pueblo was taken from a nearby pool. (*Century*, December, 1882.)

Left, ceremony of planting prayer sticks. Center, Zuni and Thunder Mountain. The Zunis moved to the mountain in times of trouble. (*Century*, May, 1883.)

Flocks of sheep returning to the pueblo. (*Century*, February, 1883.)

Zuni governor (left) and his assistants. (*Harper's*, Aug., 1875.)

Zuni man spinning, drawing the thread from a whorl held by his foot. This was rarely a man's work, but it was done at Zuni. (*Century*, Feb., 1883.)

Zuni woman weaving a belt. The other end of the loom is tied to the central support pillar of the room. (B.A.E. Annual Report, 1882.)

This view of Zuni shows adobe ovens. (*Harper's* August, 1875.)

Shrine at a sacred spring. Shrines are scattered around Zuni at springs, rocks, ruins, and mesas. (Cozzens, 1876.)

Indian and eagle cage. The eagles are kept for their feathers, which are used on masks and costumes in ceremonials. (B.A.E., 1887.)

HOUSEHOLD customs changed little at Zuni. An anthropologist's wife attempted to introduce soap and washtubs in 1879. Her demonstration was ruined because she couldn't wash properly.

"You do not understand that which you wish to teach," said her Indian student, "The missionary's wife, she keeps the water in the tub and does not make a river on the floor."

The Indian showed her how the washing should be done, but the pueblo didn't adopt the practice.

Paper-thin bread, called *hé-wé* at Zuni and *piki* in the Hopi villages, is made for special occasions. (*Century*, Feb., 1883.)

This dramatic view of Zuni emphasizes the height of both the pueblo and nearby Thunder Mountain, or Towayalane. The mountain is three miles southeast of the pueblo and 1,000 feet higher. (Thayer, 1888.)

Rooftops in the pueblos served as living room and workroom, the interior rooms being used for sleeping and storage. Here the potters are shown decorating their wares; each pueblo still has its distinctive designs. (*Century*, Dec., 1882.)

POTTERY was usually baked over dried manure fires for one or two hours.

Zuni mining party camping while on an expedition. (*Century*, Feb., 1883.)

Firing pottery. Anthropologist reported that pottery quality had declined by 1900. (*Century*, Dec., 1882.)

Zuni woman at a window. (*Harper's Weekly*, Jan. 28, 1882.)

Women grinding corn. The ground stone and corn mixture was hard on the teeth. By the 1890's all Zuni families who could afford it were buying store flour. (*Century*, February, 1883.)

In Kern's lithograph of flour grinding, the women are grinding with almost orderly precision. (Sitgreaves, 1854.)

A ZUNI marriage ceremony had a few simple rituals. The couple decided to wed, they asked permission of the girl's father. The boy ate some of the family's food and worked for them for five days. The pact was finalized with gifts of flour and a deerskin.

Zuni courtship was informal. Couples sat on the rooftops, with girl combing and washing the boy's hair. Marriage and divorce were equally casual affairs. (*Century*, May, 1883.)

Blacksmith shop, supposedly at Zuni, was drawn by one of the Kern brothers and exaggerated by the lithographer. (Sitgreaves, 1854.)

Arch and rock spires near the Zuni reservation. (Whipple, 1853-4.)

Shrine near the old pueblo of Pin-a-ua was adorned with prayer plumes. (*Jnl. of Am. Eth.*, 1891.)

Sketch of cliff dwellings near Zuni was made from a picture by the photographer who accompanied Cushing and other first Bureau of Ethnology anthropologists to the area. (*Harper's Weekly*, January 28, 1882.)

This romantic view of a Zuni priest blowing pollen at one of the pueblo's shrines was so colorful and dramatic that it was redrawn and used in many books. The painting was originally made by H. B. Mollhausen and published in Lt. Whipple's report. (Top, Cozzens, 1876; below, Cady, 1893.)

STAPLES of Zuni diet in-
cluded corn breads and
mush, eggs, chicken, beef,
goats, and mutton. Game
included deer, cottontail,
and jackrabbits.

Squash was a main
vegetable. They also made
yucca jam, ate pinon nuts
and the fruit of the prickly
pear.

The Zunis also enjoyed
corn drinks, coffee, and tea.

Women cooking breakfast in the large corner oven. (*Century*, December, 1882.)

Farm houses at one of the small villages
outside the main Zuni pueblo. (Thayer,
1888.)

"The Demon of Childhood."
Hazing by elders dressed as
gods. (*Century*, May, 1883.)

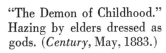

THE ZUNIS wove some blankets, but put no particular emphasis on their craftsmanship. The colors were often from the natural colors of the wool. Patterns were simply wide stripes. They traded with the Navajos for saddle blankets and the ones they wore.

The Zunis also made baskets, pots and beads. Silverwork was introduced by the Spaniards and the Zunis have become famous for this work.

Zuni woman weaving a saddle blanket. (*Century*, February, 1883.)

Artist Kern's exaggeration of Indian life shows a fancier loom. (Sitgreaves, 1854.)

Tablet dancer. (*Jnl. of Am. Eth.*, 1891.)

Ko-ko dancer of Zuni. (*Jnl. of Am. Eth.*, 1891.)

Mudhead, or clown dancer. (*Jnl. of Am. Eth.*, 1891.)

Mudheads dancing in Tablet Dance held each summer. (*Jnl. of Am. Eth.*, 1891.)

Among the New Mexico Indians, the best silver-work today is done at Zuni and Santo Domingo. Most silversmiths have workshops far more simple than the equipment shown here. (*Century*, May, 1883.)

(Below) Zuni Indians threatened to tear up Cushing's sketch pads after he drew dances such as these, but he kept them off with a knife. (*Century*, Dec., 1882.)

ANTHROPOLOGIST J. Walter Fewkes tried to record Zuni songs on wax cylinders in 1891 with an early model phonograph. Attempts to record during the actual dances were not possible because the megaphone used for a microphone would be too far away from the singers and also because they might not approve.

"I thought it best not to imperil the success of my undertaking, possibly the safety of my phonograph, by making such a display." After the dance, priests sang privately for his machine.

Ox train loaded with melons returns to Zuni. (*Century*, Dec., 1882.)

Unromantic view of a pueblo girl. (Chase, 1882.)

THE SEVEN Zuni pueblos that Coronado saw, as well as ten others, are now deserted.

After the revolt of 1680 the Zunis lived on Thunder Mountain. They returned after de Vargas' reconquest in 1692 and built the present pueblo.

The oldest section of the pueblo, on the northwest, is built on the remains of one of the earlier pueblos.

Early sketch of Zuni warriors was copied in other books. (Whipple, 1853-4.)

Emigrants stopping for supplies along the Santa Fe Trail. The "Gin Fiz" sign suggests a touch of refinement in a rough land. (*Harper's*, July, 1880.)

SANTA FE TRAIL

THE FIRST trader over the Santa Fe Trail was a Frenchman, Pedro Vial, who went from Santa Fe to St. Louis in 1792.

The first trading caravan from the U.S., led by William Becknell, arrived in Santa Fe in 1821. Wagon trade over the trail continued until the 1880's.

A caravan of wagons in the circular formation that protected them from Indian attacks. The lead wagon is ready to move out. The others can follow with a minimum of time and effort. (Inman, 1893.)

A caravan arrives in Santa Fe. Early traders were at the mercy of Mexican Governor Manuel Armijo, who charged exorbitant taxes. Traders called him "his obesity." (Gregg, 1844.)

The cattle ranch of Trinidad Romero was five miles below Las Vegas. He was a *rico* of the region, raising fruit and crops as well as cattle. (Mills, 1885.)

New Mexican trader in California. (*Harper's*, Aug., 1853.)

Mail is delivered at a frontier post office. The Butterfield route went along southern New Mexico. Other lines went along the Rio Grande and to other areas of the territory. (*Harper's Weekly*, July 4, 1874.)

Ox-drawn wagons move in a stately procession across the plains. With luck and shrewd bargaining, early traders could make more than a 600 per cent profit. (Gregg, 1849.)

New Mexican "grist mill" consisted of two stones. (Richardson, 1867.)

"Calling for the Relays" was probably sketched directly on a woodblock by Frenzeny and Tavernier. (*Harper's Weekly*, July 4, 1874.)

Conestogas and New Mexican carretas parked at a village. (Champney, 1888.)

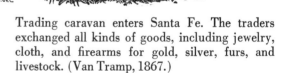

Trading caravan enters Santa Fe. The traders exchanged all kinds of goods, including jewelry, cloth, and firearms for gold, silver, furs, and livestock. (Van Tramp, 1867.)

IN THE early 1800s, trade routes went from Santa Fe to San Antonio, Texas; Tucson, Arizona; Arispe and Chihuahua, Mexico, and up into Colorado.

Trading in the more remote villages was done with mule trains like this. (Schlagintweit, 1884.)

THE FIRST regular route from Texas to California was the San Antonio and San Diego Stage Company, nicknamed the Jackass Mail. Passengers paid $200 for the ride. For one section a hundred miles west of Yuma, Arizona, they rode the jackasses. The rest of the 23 day trip was spent in a jolting stagecoach. Postage on the Jackass Mail was twenty cents per ounce, but it cost the government $60 to deliver that ounce of mail.

The Butterfield Overland Mail Co. replaced the Jackass Mail in 1858 and continued until the start of the Civil War.

(Top) A flirter is about to be surprised by a rival. (Right) A trading caravan arrives in Santa Fe. (*Harper's*, July 1880.)

Wagons cross the prairie without disturbing a group of placid pronghorn antelope. (*Harper's*, September, 1862.)

Pack train camped in the mountains. The *arrieros*, mule drivers, are getting ready to move out. (Gregg, 1849.)

Aristocratic New Mexican don. (*Harper's*, July, 1880.)

A *baile* (ball) or *fandago* was held on the slightest excuse—or no excuse at all. The dancing, staid by modern standards, astonished some puritan Americans but not the average soldier! (Triplett, 1885.)

"A Saturday Noon in a Southwestern Town", sketched directly on a wood block by Frenzeny and Tavernier for later engraving in the *Harper's* plant. When the artists sketched on wood, a "Z" or "N" was sometimes reversed. In this case, an "N". (*Harper's Weekly*, July 25, 1874.)

NEW TOWNS AND OLD

THE FIRST TOWNS in New Mexico were, of course, the Indian pueblos. When the first Spanish colonists arrived they settled near the pueblos. Later settlers stuck to the rivers and streams that gave them a dependable water supply. Isolated ranchos grew into small villages and, by the early 1700s towns such as Santa Cruz, Armijo and Los Lunas were scattered along the Rio Grande valley.

When hordes of Anglos arrived after the Civil War, new towns sprang up overnight. Mining towns such as Pinos Altos, Georgetown, Silver City, Chloride, Winston, and others in the southwestern section thrived for years.

In the north, Cimarron, Elizabethtown, Arroyo Hondo, Las Vegas, Bonanza, and others were supported by mines, the stock business, or traders.

Cattle and agriculture boomed Lincoln, Roswell, Tularosa, and other towns in the southwestern part of New Mexico.

Some of the old towns had gloriously optimistic names: Acme, Avalon, Park City, Queen, Brilliant. There were also towns named Lizard, Tin Pan, Toboggan Gulch, Hardscrabble, High Lonesome, and Whiskey Creek.

One town tried both types of names. Badgerville changed its name to Hope. It didn't help. Plans to develop the town failed and it never grew. Today it has a population of about 100.

The Atchison, Topeka and Santa Fe brought new life to the territory in 1879 and a whole new breed of towns—the railheads—were born. As the railroad was built south, and later west, each railhead became a quick metropolis complete with gambling houses, restaurants on wheels, honkytonks, and hotels. Many of the towns were soon passed by and forgotten. Otero, for instance, lasted only six months. Wallace, Waldo, Florida, and other towns had their moment of glory and then were forgotten.

Some new towns began when local landowners held out for high prices. Rather than pay through the nose for land at Las Vegas and Albuquerque, railroad officials bought cheaper lots about a mile from the towns. Railroad stations were built and new business districts grew up about them.

Some of the railroad towns, such as Deming, Vaughn, Alamogordo, and Lordsburg, are still thriving.

Oil and the railroads were important factors in shifting New Mexico's population in the late 1800s and early 1900s. In the 1870s, southwestern towns such as Mogollon, Tyrone, and Shakespeare had relatively large populations. As the mines played out and these towns became deserted, Roswell, Carlsbad, Artesia, Hobbs, and other towns on the southeastern side began to gain population. Cattle and agriculture became more important there as railroads provided easier access to the markets.

Then, in the 20th century, oil and potash were discovered. Except for Albuquerque and Santa Fe, the southeastern cities are now generally the most populous in the state.

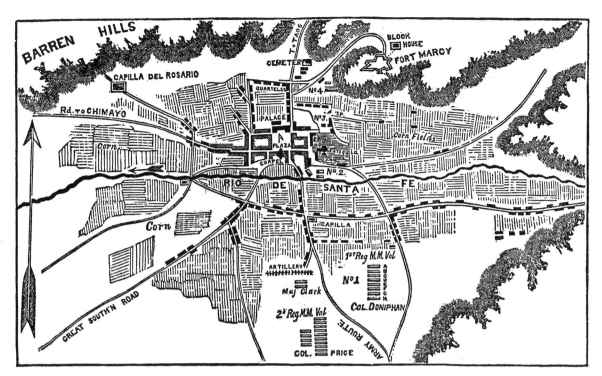

Map of Santa Fe just after its occupation by Kearny in 1846. (Hughes, 1850.)

Santa Fe as it was just after the American occupation. The new Fort Marcy is on the low hill where the flag is seen in this picture. (Abert, 1847.)

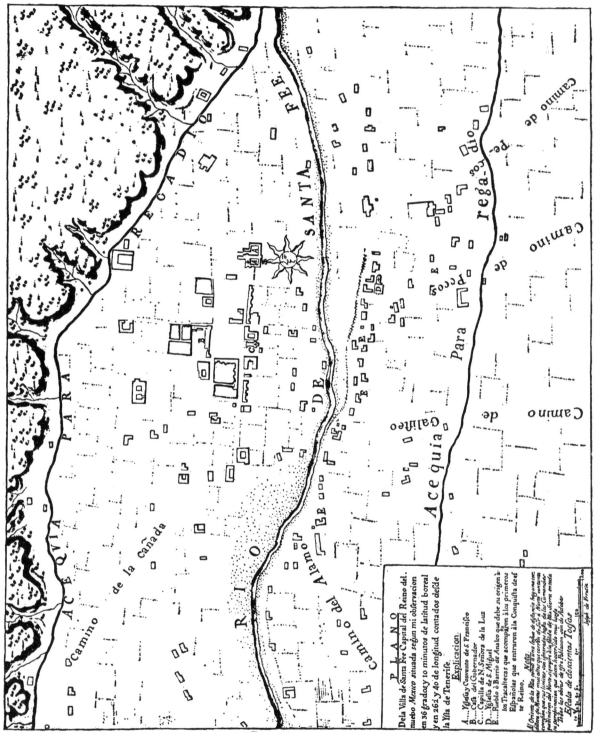

The earliest known map of Santa Fe, drawn by Jose de Urrutia, around 1766-68 (Adams.)

East side of the Santa Fe plaza. (Beadle, 1873.)

Santa Fe is a placid agricultural town in this old drawing. (*Harper's Weekly*, Nov. 13, 1879.)

Stagecoach arrives at the Exchange Hotel on San Francisco street. (*Harper's*, April, 1880.)

Oñaté Trail, Leading North   Baldy Peak.   Cañon of the Rio Santa Fe.

Presbyterian Church.   Hospital.   Santa Fe Academy.   Santa Fe Range.   The Fort.   Palace Hotel.   Old Spanish Government Palace.

Soldiers' Barracks.   H'dq'rs of the Post.   Residence of Gen. L. P. Bradley, Com'dg Dist.

Officers' Quarters.   Officers' Quarters.   General Offices.

Grant Street, looking North.   Palace Avenue, looking East.

The further of the three residences facing Grant Street was the quarters of Ex-President Grant and family, when they visited Santa Fe, in 1880.

HEADQUARTERS MILITARY DISTRICT OF NEW MEXICO.

FORT MARCY. (Santa Fe.)

Map of the Military District of Santa Fe. Few of the buildings shown here are still standing. (Ritch, 1885.)

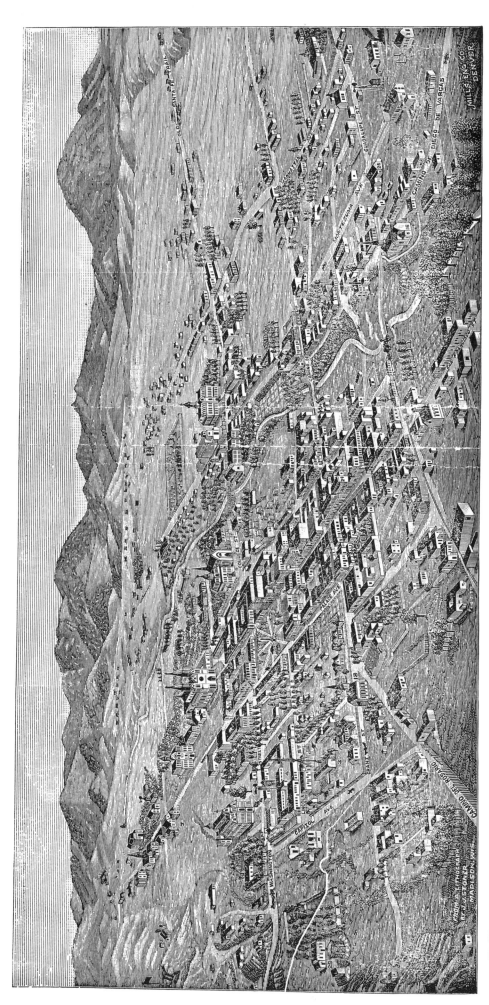

CITY OF SANTA FE, NEW MEXICO.
(COPYRIGHTED.)

Presented by the Bureau of Immigration, New Mexico.

Ft. Marcy.   Episcopal Church.   Cañon of the Rio Santa Fe.   San Miguel Cemetery.   El Atalaya.
St. Vincent's Hospital.   Cathedral San Francisco (See of Santa Fe.)   Bishop's Garden.   Camping Ground U. S. Army, Aug. 18, 1846.   Santa Fe Trail.
Palace Hotel.   Academy and Convent Sisters Loretto.   San Miguel Church and College.   Rio de Santa Fe.
Masonic and Odd Fellows' Cemetery.   Spanish Government Palace.   Plaza and Center of Business.   Territorial Penitentiary.
Gas Works.   State House Grounds.   U. S. Military Reservation, H'd Qrs. Dist. N. M.   Congregational Church.
Tri-Centenary Celebration Grounds, 1883.   Presbyterian Church.   Texas, Santa Fe and Northern R. R.   A. T. and S. F. R. R. Depot.
Guadalupe Church.   Methodist Church.   U. S. Indian School. (Gov. Vigil Place.

Birds-eye view of Santa Fe in 1882. The general layout of the town may still be recognized and some of the buildings identified are still there. (Ritch, 1882-3.)

One of Santa Fe's most popular subjects for visiting artists is this adobe house, said to be the oldest inhabited one in the U.S. Part of it may have been built by the Indians who lived in Santa Fe before the Spaniards arrived, but other parts were added later. (*Harper's Weekly*, Nov. 13, 1879.)

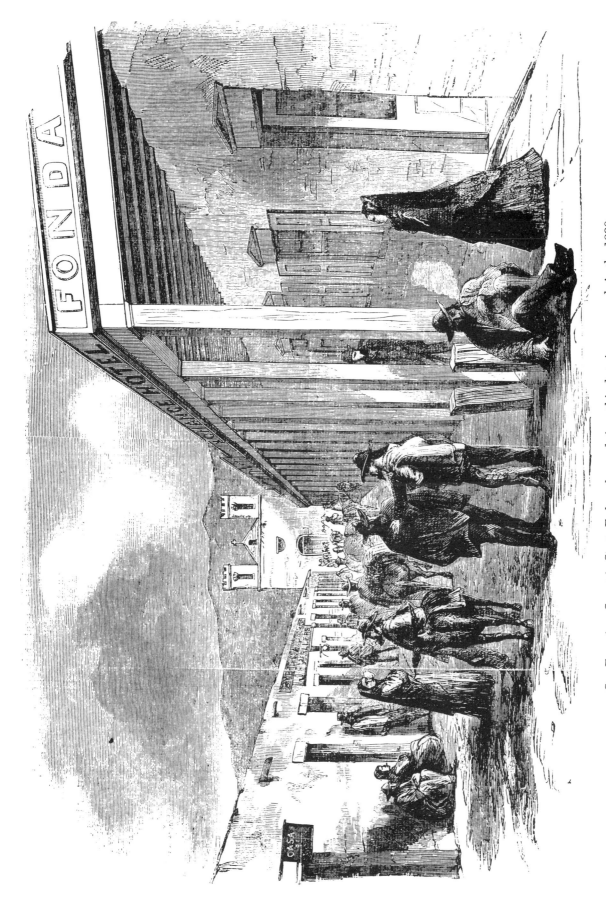

San Francisco Street in Santa Fe has changed since this drawing was made in the 1880s. St. Francis Cathedral looks about the same, but the Exchange Hotel has been replaced by La Fonda. (*Harper's Weekly,* Apr. 21, 1886.)

Pencil sketch of the Palace of Governors was made by Gov. Lew Wallace. (Wallace, 1889.)

GAMBLING was one of Santa Fe's main industries, and monte its most popular attraction. Dollars, pesos, Spanish doubloons and gold dust were all legal tender. Players habitually kept a bowie knife or pistol handy to satisfy any complaints.

Dona Tules (Gertrudes Barcelo,) Santa Fe's foremost lady gambler. (*Harper's*, April, 1854.)

Patrons in the gambling house of Dona Tules in Santa Fe. (*Harper's*, April, 1854.)

This view of Santa Fe (right) makes it appear very populous. Design of the Palace of Governors shows brickwork front. (Thayer, 1888.)

Palace (center) in the 1890's in territorial style. (*Harper's Weekly*, July 19, 1890.)

Palace and Santa Fe's tree-shaded plaza. The palace has since been remodeled to its more original Pueblo form. (Ladd, 1891.)

Catron Building on the east side of Santa Fe Plaza is still used by the Catron law firm and the design of its upper story remains unchanged. (Frost, 1894.)

Street scene in Santa Fe, 1885. A stagecoach turns from what is today Shelby street onto San Francisco street. The Exchange Hotel is now La Fonda. Seligman's store has gone, but its successor recently rebuilt the *portal* or roof over the sidewalk. (Ritch, 1885.)

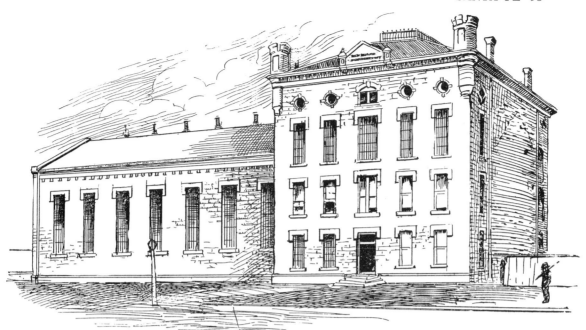

The old Territorial Penitentiary (above) was near Cerrillos Road and Cordova Road in Santa Fe. It was recently torn down. Santa Fe was given its choice of the
penitentiary or the state university; it chose the prison.
(Frost, 1894.)

Caramba! A burro can be ornery at times! (Beadle,
1873.)

The Presbyterian Mission School (below) was a Santa
Fe landmark. (Frost, 1894.)

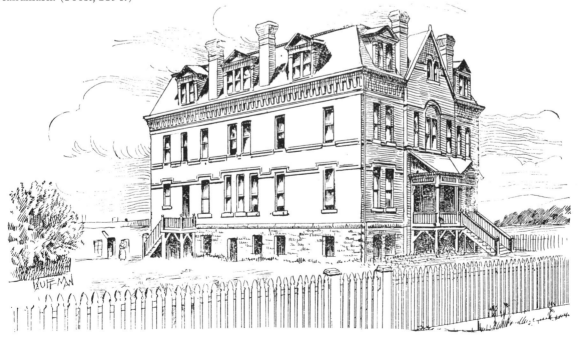

Gambling in Santa Fe was both popular and legal. (Richardson, 1867.)

State capitol was started in 1900. It is now part of the state office building. (State letterhead, 1917.)

THE TERRITORIAL style of architecture popular today is a mixture of pueblo adobe and Californian. It is a relatively late blending of traditional materials and modern methods.

Most of the larger buildings built during territorial days were inappropriate-looking but relatively functional buildings in Victorian.

Family making tortillas. (Gregg, 1849.)

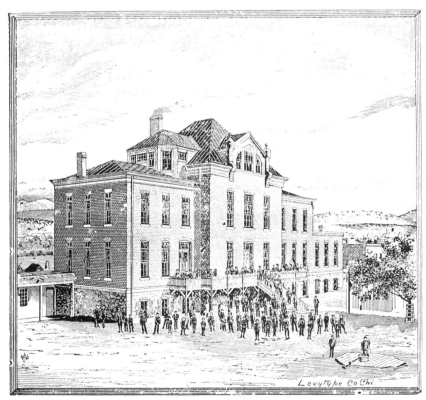

Class building of St. Michael's College on College St. in Santa Fe. (Frost, 1894.)

Easterner who married a New Mexican girl introduces a friend to his new horde of relatives. (Beadle, 1873.)

New Mexico's capitol from 1884 to 1892. (*Ladd*, 1891.)

This is apparently the architect's drawing for the capitol authorized by the Territorial Legislature. Only the section on the right was built. (Ritch, 1885.)

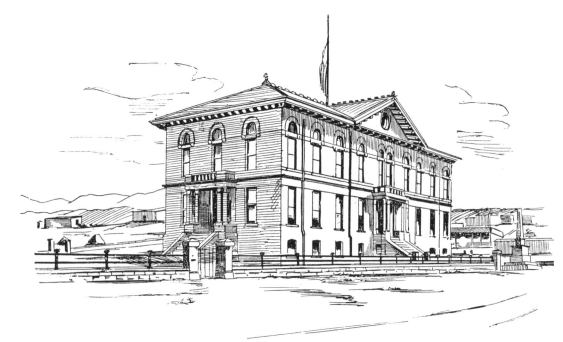

Old Federal Building on Lincoln Avenue (above) was built shortly after the Civil War. (Frost, 1894.)

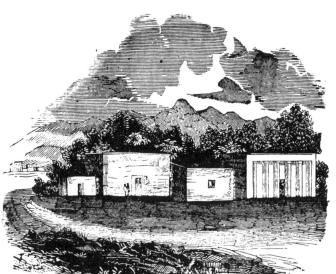

This early sketch of Santa Fe was probably drawn by one who had never seen the town. (Frost, 1851.)

Indian School in Santa Fe (below) is now the New Mexico School for the Deaf. (Frost, 1894.)

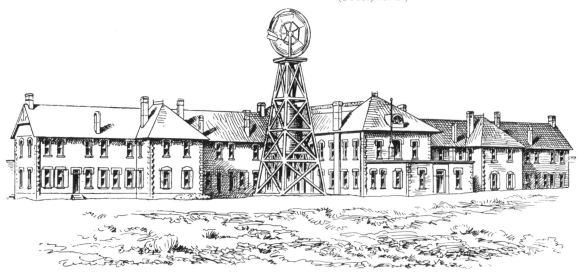

A bustling Santa Fe street. (Higgins, 1896.)

J. Gold's Free Museum (below,) is one of the older surviving buildings in Santa Fe. The city attempts to save its old buildings through historical zoning, but some buildings outside the zones have been torn down.

San Francisco Street in the 1890s. The "Free Museum" is now a trading post. (*Harper's Weekly*, July 19, 1890.)

Santa Fe in the 1890s. The large building on the right was New Mexico's brand new capitol. It burned down a year after this picture was published. (Ladd, 1891.)

Early home of the First National Bank, Santa Fe, founded by Lucien Maxwell and others in 1870 as the first bank in New Mexico. (Ritch, 1882-3.)

The Spiegelberg Building in Santa Fe. (Ritch, 1885.)

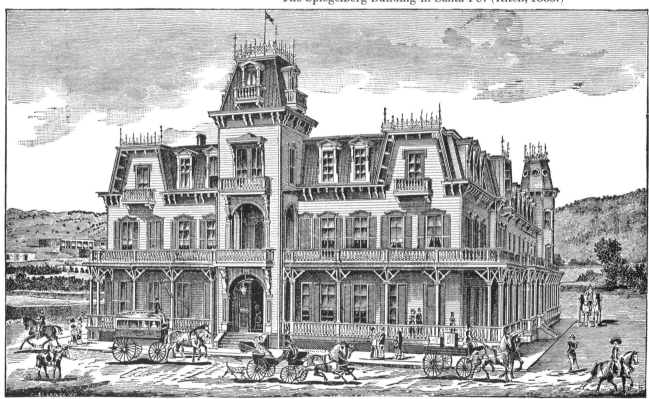

Palace Hotel in Santa Fe stood near today's City Hall on Washington Ave. (Ritch, 1885.)

Santa Fe was a cosmopolitan city in the 1880s and '90s. The hotels were prosperous and ornate. The best food was shipped in by rail. Beautiful furniture, statues, pianos, and other symbols of gracious living were all in evidence in the better homes. The stores sold an amazing variety of goods, from pins to wagons. Bacon was about 11 cents per pound. Coffee mills sold for $5.50 per dozen. Mixed and fancy candy was 17 cents per pound.

The home of Abraham Staab on Palace Avenue has had its face lifted since the 1800s. It is now a large motel, but some of the interior remains the same. (Ritch, 1885.)

DeVargas Street and San Miguel Church. (Ritch, 1885.)

Pioneer merchant Levi Spiegelberg hosted President Rutherford B. Hayes at this home in Santa Fe in 1880. (Ritch, 1885.)

ARCHBISHOP LAMY and the St. Francis Cathedral gained national recognition through Willa Cather's novel *Death Comes for the Archbishop.*

Religious ceremony in the streets of Santa Fe. (*Harper's*, July, 1880.)

Archbishop Lamy and the St. Francis Cathedral as he originally planned it. The tall towers were never finished. (Ritch, 1885.)

View of Santa Fe from Fort Marcy. (*Harper's Weekly*, July 14, 1883.)

Loretto chapel has famous miraculous circular staircase. (*Harper's*, April, 1880.)

Loretto Academy in Santa Fe, closed in 1968, founded by Sister Blandina. (Ritch, 1885.)

Interior of St. Francis Cathedral. (*Harper's*, April, 1880.)

Roof of St. Francis Cathedral during its construction. (*Harper's*, April, 1880.)

San Miguel Church.
(Sweetser, 1891.)

SAN MIGUEL church has been changed several times since it was built. Triple-stepped tower atop it was destroyed by a storm in 1872.

"Oldest House in Santa Fe." (*Harper's Weekly*, Sept. 7, 1889.)

San Miguel Church as it appeared in the 1870s. (Roberts, 1885.)

Wooden-wheeled carreta was drawn by oxen. Probably no working example of either is left in New Mexico. (Peters, 1874.)

San Miguel Church and College Street in the 1880s. To the right, with cupola, is St. Michael's College. (*Harper's Weekly*, July 14, 1883.)

View of San Miguel church from the side, by a German traveler. Most early views were taken from the front. The figures are walking down what is now DeVargas street. (Schlagintweit, 1884.)

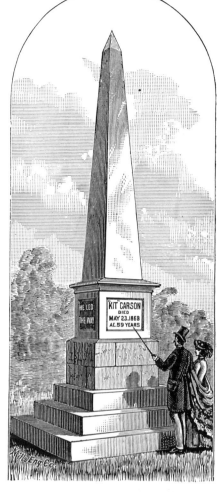

Monument to Kit Carson still stands in front of the old Federal Building. (Ritch, 1885.)

Soldier's Monument to Civil War veterans is in the Santa Fe plaza. (*Harper's Weekly*, July 19, 1890.)

San Miguel Church and DeVargas St. The new State Library now stands where the building on the right is in this picture. (Frost, 1894.)

IN THE last years of the 19th century, Santa Fe settled down to outgrow its earlier, rowdier days.

Business blossomed. The town had a population of 6,038 (excluding Indians,) in 1890. It was the largest single town in the territory.

One highlight of those days was the tertio-millenial celebration held in 1883 to commemorate Coronado's expedition of 1540. Chartered Pullman cars brought visitors from as far away as New England to watch the festivities. The fiesta lasted 33 days and was considered a great success, though its backers lost money.

New high school was Santa Fe's pride in the 1890s. (Frost, 1894.)

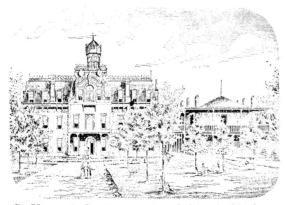

St. Vincent's Sanitarium, founded by Archbishop Lamy and the Sisters of Charity of Cincinnati. (Frost, 1894.)

St. Catherine's Indian School
in Santa Fe. (Sweetser, 1891.)

Outdoor market near the plaza
in Santa Fe. (*Harper's*, April,
1880.)

Students listening to the padre.
(*Harper's*, April, 1880.)

THE SANTA FE plaza has been
the scene of both peace and
action for more than 350
years. In 1680, besieged
Spanish colonists slowly
trudged out of the plaza to
escape the rebelling Pueblo
Indians. Religious and
patriotic celebrations here
marked Mexico's indepen-
dence from Spain in 1821. The
plaza was the busy end of the
Santa Fe Trail for many years.
It is now a quiet oasis in the
midst of bustling auto traffic—
but still the cultural center of
Santa Fe.

A bustling spring morning on
the plaza in Santa Fe. (*Harper's*,
April, 1880.)

Early sketch of Santa Fe, with mission in foreground. Flag in the distance is atop Fort Marcy. Right foreground is now the site of an urban renewal project. (Davis, 1857.)

Wood peddlers brought burro-loads of fragrant piñon logs to market in Santa Fe's plaza. (*Harper's*, April, 1880.)

When the first traders came over the Trail, Santa Fe was the largest town in New Mexico. (Howe, 1852.)

The first Protestant church in New Mexico was this one built in 1853. (*Harper's Weekly*, Nov. 13, 1879.)

THE FIRST PRESBYTERIAN CHURCH celebrated its centennial in 1968. The Loretto Academy closed and put its property up for sale in that year.

View of Santa Fe from the roof of St. Michael's. (Sweetser, 1891.)

Parroquia church in Santa Fe was built on the edge of the Barrio Analco, the original Indian pueblo. (Drake, 1887.)

First Presbyterian Church was built in 1881. (Ritch, 1885.)

A "grand entree into Santa Fe" was the description given for this vignette by an early traveler. (*Harper's*, April, 1854.)

Making cane seat chairs. Most of the things made in early 19th century New Mexico would be considered the products of crafts rather than industries. (Higgins, 1896.)

Seal of New Mexico. Left, the original Territorial seal, now used by the Historical Society of New Mexico; center, an elaborate seal from the Blue Book of the Territory, 1882; right, modern seal, adopted after statehood in 1912.

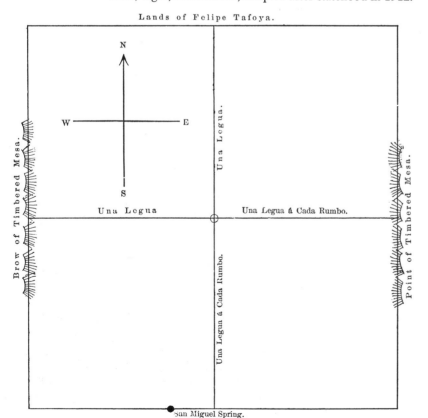

Spanish land grants in New Mexico were made by the governor at Santa Fe in the name of the king, with final title retained by the king. After annexation by the United States, a legal procedure was established by which old titles could be validated and continued. Sketch map here shows boundaries of the "San Miguel grant, in the province of Navajo." Later known as the Bartolome Fernandez Grant, it is now part of a big ranch owned by Floyd Lee at San Mateo, near Grants. (U.S. Govt. Doc., 1874.)

Sleepy plaza of Albuquerque in the 1850s. This plaza was actually to the west of today's Old Town Plaza. (Davis, 1857.)

ALBUQUERQUE

Except for surrounding wall, San Felipe Church looks much the same today. (Sweetser, 1891.)

Wall around the plaza was added later. (Sweetser, 1891)

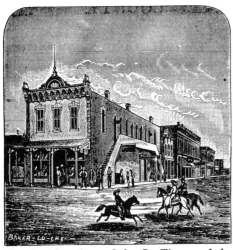

This building housed the St. Elmo and the White Elephant saloons. It was where the Sunshine Building on Second and Central is today. (Ritch, 1885.)

One of several old haciendas in Albuquerque. (*Harper's,* April, 1885.)

Many of Albuquerque's older residents, like the Hunings, Armijos, and Blueher's, lived in Old Town but had businesses in New Town. Visitors from New Town to Joe Badaracco's Summer Garden and the county offices on the plaza were common. In the 1880s, a horse-drawn trolley operated between the two areas. The trolley, restored, now hauls tourists around Old Town in the summer.

Franz Huning's home was a showplace of Albuquerque. It stood near 14th and Central until the 1950s. Some of the lumber for the house came from Illinois, other materials were brought from England. (Haines, 1891.)

View of the mesa at the mouth of Tijeras Canyon, with insets showing Albuquerque scenes, was sketched for a local humor magazine. (*Adobeland*, Aug., 1891.)

Early view of Albuquerque and the Sandia Mountains. (Whipple, 1856.)

New Mexico carreta. (Chase, 1882.)

First bridge across Rio Grande at Albuquerque was 1,600 feet long. (Ritch, 1882-3.)

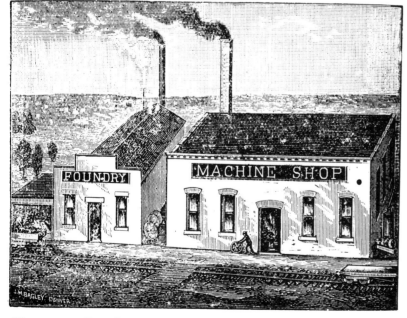

Albuquerque Foundry and Machine Works is still in business at the same location on South Broadway in Albuquerque. (Ritch, 1882-3.)

Bernalillo County Court House was just off Central Ave. (then Railroad Ave.) near Old Town. (Letterhead, 1891.)

San Felipe Hotel stood on the corner of Fifth and Gold, where the newest Federal Building is today. (Haines, 1891.)

NEW TOWN sprang up like grass after a desert rain when the railroad arrived in 1880. Many of the buildings of the 1880s and 1890s are still in use, although some of them have been remodeled.

The San Felipe Hotel became the Elks Club and lasted until 1961. The Rose Building at 120 Gold S.W. is still in use after more than seventy years.

Hill St. (now Elm St.) marked the eastern edge of the town in the 1890s and there were hardly more than two dozen houses between Tenth Street and Old Town.

This Victorian house at Los Lunas was the home Manuel B. Otero, later of Solomon Luna. It was built in the 1880s and is still occupied. (Carruth, 1897.)

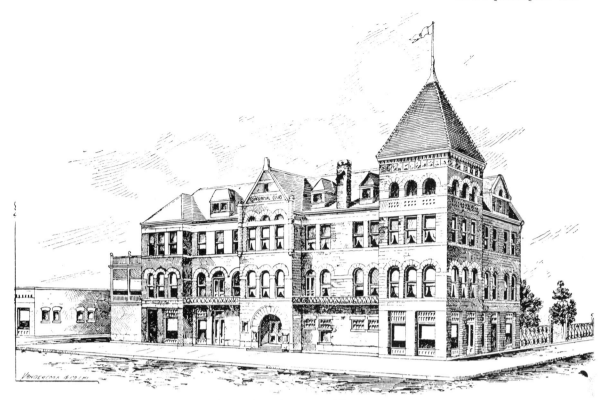

Commercial Club was on the corner of Fourth and Gold in Albuquerque, where the Simms Building is today. (Frost, 1894.)

The old Albuquerque *Morning Journal* office was at 312 Gold SW. (Ritch, 1885.)

A flour mill, "Molino de la Glorieta," stood near the Huning home. It was near the corner of today's Central and Laguna Blvd., SW. (*Harper's*, April, 1885.)

Original building of the present University of New Mexico. Remodeled, it is now Hodgin Hall. (Frost, 1894.)

The women of Albuquerque who lived on the west side of the Rio Grande didn't wait for the small ferry when they wanted to cross the river to attend Mass. They simply pulled up their skirts and waded across. (Beadle, 1873.)

The latest Victorian gingerbread and a widow's walk decorated the M.A. Otero home in Bernalillo. (Ritch, 1885.)

LAS VEGAS

LAS VEGAS began with the awarding of a land grant to Don Luis Maria Cabeza de Baca and his seventeen children in 1823. The family was soon driven out by hostile Indians.

In 1832, Santa Fe trader Josiah Gregg noticed one small hovel where the town stands today. In 1835, 29 men petitioned for the grant title formerly held by the de Bacas.

The town they built was a monotonous collection of mud huts that made a poor impression on travelers seeing New Mexico for the first time.

When Kearny's Army of the West reached Las Vegas in 1846, one of his first acts was to climb atop one of the houses on the plaza and read a message proclaiming New Mexico part of the U.S.

The new, raw town of East Las Vegas was built and ready for the first railroad train when it arrived on July 4th, 1879.

Two who greeted the train were Manuel Barela and Giovanni Dugi. They were dangling by their necks from the town windmill on the plaza.

Barela had killed a couple of men while testing his marksmanship by shooting off their coat-buttons—from the front. Dugi had killed two men "by accident," he said, when his revolver fired while he was demonstrating the road agent's spin.

The local vigilantes held a necktie party for the two. They pinned a note to Dugi's coat. "This was no accident."

The railroad helped boom the new town. It also brought a gang of killers, con men and robbers who ran the town for about six months. They decamped before the vigilantes could use them to decorate tree limbs.

The new town then settled down and began to thrive. The two towns, East and West Las Vegas, remained separate until 1968, when the citizens voted to combine them.

First house in Las Vegas was built by Manuel Romero in 1833. (Wilson, 1880.)

Old Catholic church at Las Vegas was on the northwest corner of the plaza. (Wilson, 1880.)

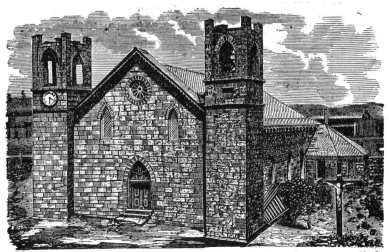
Our Lady of Sorrows Church in old Vegas had no heat, was called a "magnificent refrigerator." (Wilson, 1880.)

Ward and Tamme's Opera House was at 320-2 Railroad Ave. (All pictures on this page show Las Vegas, from Mills, 1885.)

First National Bank still stands on the Old Las Vegas Plaza on the corner of National and Market. The other buildings shown on this page are now gone.

Street car stables were on the west corner of Main and 12th streets.

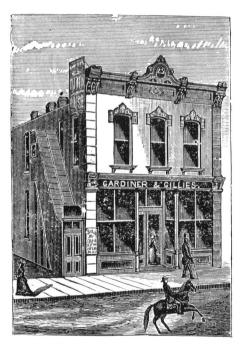

Wells, Fargo and Co. express office was on Lincoln between Grand and Railroad.

Optic Building was on Lincoln near the corner of 7th and Grand.

LAS VEGAS got its first growth through the Santa Fe trade. Mining, stock raising and agriculture later brought more business. In the 1880s, Las Vegas rivaled Santa Fe and Albuquerque in size and importance.

West Las Vegas as it looked in 1880. (Wilson, 1880.)

Main store of the Ilfeld Co., on the Plaza in Las Vegas. (Letterhead, 1899.)

Ilfeld's wholesale warehouse. This firm was one of the largest in the territory. (Letterhead, 1899.)

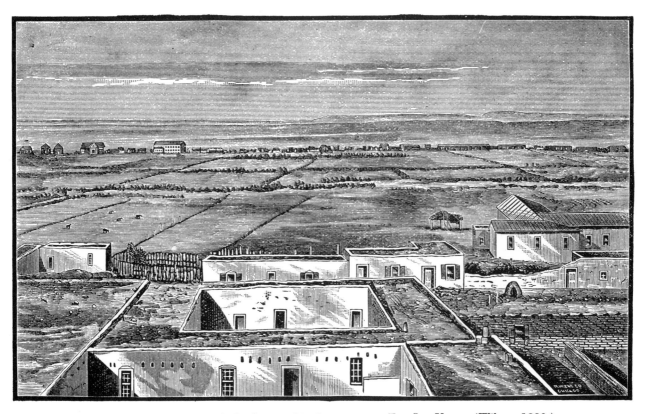

Las Vegas in 1880. In the background is the new town, East Las Vegas. (Wilson, 1880.)

Burros carried everything and everybody along rough New Mexico trails and through crowded streets. (Wilson, 1880.)

Adobe homes in the southern section of Old Las Vegas. (Wilson, 1880.)

Haciendas owned by *ricos* were often shaded by surrounding cottonwoods. (Ladd, 1891.)

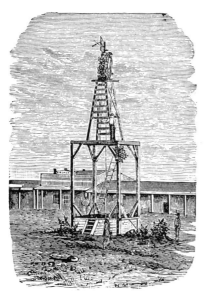

Windmill stood in the Old Las Vegas Plaza. It was torn down in 1880 after citizens complained that the men hung from it might have contaminated the water. (Wilson, 1880.)

The burros in this exaggerated drawing seem to be doing a balancing act—carrying barrels, wood, and tremendous loads of hay without pack saddles. No burro would submit to such an indignity. (Richardson, 1867.)

LUXURY SPA OF THE WEST

NEW MEXICO has been a mecca for health seekers for many years. Fifty years ago the high towns such as Las Vegas, Santa Fe, and Albuquerque had small suburbs of tents where "lungers" waited either to die or recover. Many who came west for their health, including Sen. Clinton P. Anderson, lived to become prominent citizens. Other famous health seekers included Gov. William Thornton, Sen. Bronson Cutting, and Dr. John H. (Doc) Holliday.

THE MONTEZUMA Hot Springs Hotel was started in 1879 and sold to the Santa Fe Railway in 1880.

VISITORS at the hotel included Generals Grant and Sherman, President Hayes, and Jesse James (who said he was a railroad man.)

The Montezuma burned down in 1884 and was replaced by the Phoenix, but even the new hotel was locally called the Montezuma.

The magnificent old Phoenix still stands in a wooded canyon near Las Vegas. It is now a seminary for Mexican priests.

Old Phoenix Hotel looks about the same today as it did when this was drawn eighty years ago. (Thayer, 1888.)

Fountains and spacious grounds were laid out in front of the Phoenix. (*Las Vegas Hot Springs*, n.d.)

Porches at the Phoenix overlooked the green Gallinas Canyon. (*Las Vegas Hot Springs,* n.d.)

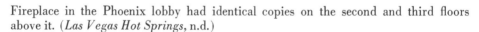

Fireplace in the Phoenix lobby had identical copies on the second and third floors above it. (*Las Vegas Hot Springs,* n.d.)

Plush dining room at the Phoenix offered trout, venison, partridge, grouse, duck, crab, turtle, shrimp. (*Las Vegas Hot Springs*, n.d.)

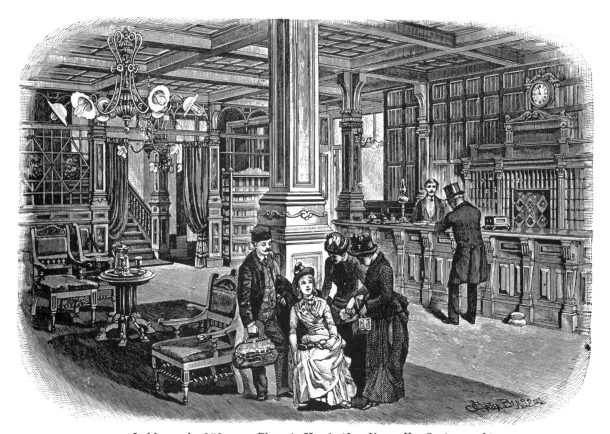

Lobby at the 172-room Phoenix Hotel. (*Las Vegas Hot Springs*, n.d.)

Gallinas Canyon, west of Las Vegas, seen from porch of the Phoenix Hotel. (*Las Vegas Hot Springs*, n.d.)

Phoenix Hotel nestled in the canyon. It was surrounded by pines, bath houses, bridle paths. (*Las Vegas Hot Springs*, n.d.)

Don Fernando de Taos, the Spanish town of Taos, was settled in the early 1600s. It has long been a trading center, beginning in prehistoric times when Taos Pueblo Indians traded with the Apaches, Utes, Navajo, Comanches, and Pawnees. The first official annual Taos trade fair was held at Don Fernando de Taos in 1723. (Davis, 1857.)

TAOS

THE TOWN of Taos today shows little evidence of its violent past. It has survived the Pueblo Revolt, the Taos Revolt, Indian raids, intrigues, and the riotous yearly rendezvous of the early mountain men.

Ruins of the Catholic mission at Taos. It was burned during the 1847 Taos Revolt. (Schlagintweit, 1884.)

A fanciful sketch of "Kit Carson's home in Taos." The home, now an excellent museum, probably never looked like this, nor did the town behind it. (Peters, 1858.)

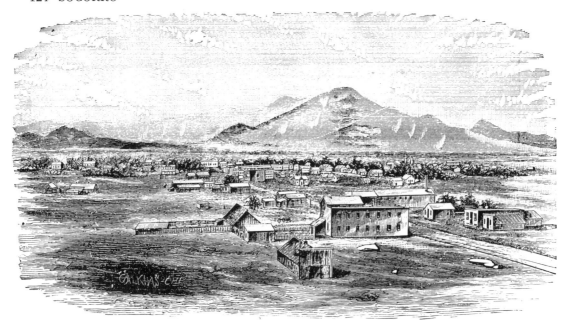

The town of Socorro nestles at the base of Socorro Mountain. The town began in 1628 when a mission was built at a Piro pueblo there. Socorro has seen the Pueblo Revolt, the Civil War, cattle drives, and the violence of frontier life. The nearby mines are closed, but the town survives on trade and agriculture. (Ritch, 1882-3.)

The smelter at Socorro processed silver from the mountains. The silver was discovered in 1867, and the town soon boomed to become the biggest in New Mexico in the 1880's. (Ritch, 1885.)

Courthouse at Mora is still used. (Letterhead, 1890.)

Chaves County courthouse was built in 1890. It has since been replaced. (Letterhead, 1891.)

San Miguel County courthouse in Las Vegas' new town. (Letterhead, 1889.)

Windsor Hotel in Socorro was on East Manzanares
St. (Ritch, 1885.)

Original building of New Mexico School of
Mines at Socorro. The school opened in 1892.
(Letterhead, 1894).

Another view of the School of Mines, now the New
Mexico Institute of Mining and Technology. (Frost,
1894.)

The town of Cubero, near Laguna, as it was in the 1850's. (Davis, 1857.)

A street in the village of Los Lunas. (Frost, 1894.)

Wool warehouse at Springer. (Ritch, 1882-3.)

Upper Cubero. The pillar in the background is, like Cabezon and Shiprock, the core of an ancient volcano. (Davis, 1857.)

Peaceful town of Algodones. The town is still peaceful, but no longer on the main trail to Santa Fe as it was in the 1800s. (Beadle, 1873.)

Old mill at Chamita, near Abiquiu. (Sweetser, 1891.)

Raton, seen from Goat Hill. (Sweetser, 1891.)

Ojo Caliente resort above Espanola. The springs had been used by Indians for many years before the Spaniards arrived. (Ritch, 1885.)

The town of Eddy, organized in 1889, is now
Carlsbad. (Ladd, 1891.)

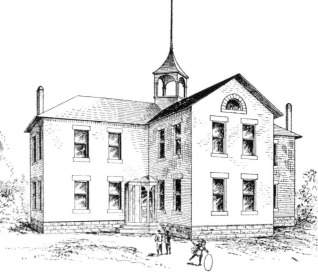

First school building in Carlsbad. (Frost, 1894.)

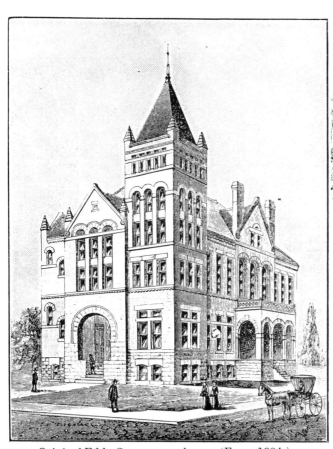

Original Eddy County courthouse. (Frost, 1894.)

Irrigation projects at Carlsbad. (Sweetser, 1891.)

Sierra County courthouse was built in Hillsboro in 1892. It is now one of the ruins in that ghost town. (Sierra County letterhead, 1900.)

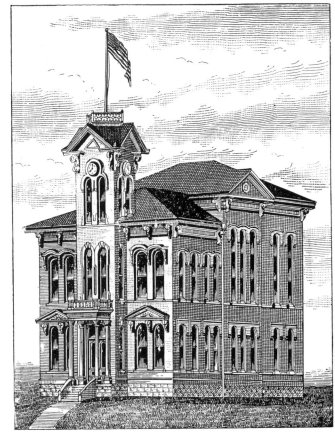

First agricultural college building at Las Cruces, built in the early 1890's, was Hadley Hall. It was named for the founder of the college. (Frost, 1894.)

Irrigation ditches bring water to the crops. (Wood, 1889.)

Beehive shaped oven, or *horno*, is seen at Indian pueblos. (Thayer, 1888.)

Grist mill. One of the few examples left in New Mexico is the large and historic old mill at Ruidoso. (Ritch, 1885.)

The gardens of Isleta, a peaceful oasis along the Rio Grande. (*Harper's,* April, 1885.)

TRADITIONAL adobe homes, such as the one shown on this page, sometimes had walls three feet thick. Adobe is a fine insulation, keeping the house warm in winter and cool in summer. Long vigas support layers of smaller branches and twigs. Adobe is piled on top for the roof. Carved beams instead of vigas and ornate corbels were sometimes used for their decorative qualities.

Square adobe houses enclosed a large, cool central plaza in typical New Mexican homes. (*Harper's,* April, 1885.)

The town of Bluewater, near Grants, was an isolated village until the 1880s, when a railroad was built from Albuquerque to the West Coast. (Beadle, 1873.)

THE VILLAGE of Santa Cruz de la Cañada was settled by Don Juan de Oñate's immigrants in 1592. After the Pueblo Revolt the village was occupied by Indians. The Spaniards returned in 1695 and built a new village about a mile away from the earlier one.

Two small battles were fought near Santa Cruz, one in the revolt of 1837 against Gov. Perez and another during the Taos Revolt of 1847.

Some settlers lived in dugouts covered with dirt or pieces of dried marsh grass. (*Harper's Weekly*, Sept. 7, 1889.)

Emigrant to New Mexico is "out here for his health." (Chase, 1882.)

The old church at Santa Cruz was built in 1733. It is still used. (*Harper's*, May, 1885.)

Church and shrine at Santa Cruz stand on the main plaza. (Ritch, 1885.)

Wild fandango at Santa Fe. (Beadle, 1873.)

The town of Valencia, south of Albuquerque, and a nearby lava-topped mesa named Tomé Hill. (Emory, 1848.)

Settlers were induced to come to New Mexico by land offices brochures showing pictures of a "modern agricultural ranch" such as this. Railroads, rivers, and forests were emphasized. (Ritch, 1885.)

GHOST TOWN

LAKE VALLEY began early in the 1880's when miners found gold in the area. It grew quickly from a crude camp to a prosperous town. The ore was worth as much as $1,000 a ton. The veins of gold, silver, lead, and manganese were usually at a depth of only forty feet or less.

The town died in the financial panic of 1893.

Smelting works at Lake Valley. The Bridal Chamber mine there once produced $3 million in horn silver ore in six months. (Thayer, 1888.)

The mines around Lake Valley were lode mines, unlike the open pit copper mines at Santa Rita. (Ritch, 1885.)

The town of Lake Valley, west of Hatch, is one of several old mining camps in that area that are now ghost towns. (Ritch, 1882-3.)

Soldiers in the Mexican War had no travelling laundry; instead they halted for a "camp washing day" as in this sketch from the journal of William H. Richardson. (1848.)

Bent's Fort on the Arkansas River was not in New Mexico but it was the principal stopping place on the Santa Fe Trail. It is now being restored by the National Park Service. (Inman, 1893.)

Members of the Texan Santa Fe expedition of 1841 are marched south to Mexico City after their capture. (Brown, 1906.)

Members of Col. Jacob Snively's 1843 Texan expedition to Santa Fe find their horses stampeding through their camp. The 107 men were captured by Capt. Philip St. George Cooke of the U.S. Army near today's Dodge City. (Sage, 1854.)

WAR WITH MEXICO

AN UNPOPULAR WAR between the U.S. and Mexico began on May 13, 1846. Generals Zachary Taylor and Winfield Scott moved on Texas and Mexico City. Gen. Stephen Watts Kearny and his Army of the West headed for New Mexico.

The army arrived in Las Vegas on August 15th. Kearny climbed atop a roof on the plaza and proclaimed New Mexico part of the U.S. Three days later, after Gov. Manuel Armijo had placed his troops for battle and then escaped south to Mexico, Kearny marched through a dispersed Mexican army and took Santa Fe.

Kearny marched on to California. He left Col. Alexander Doniphan in charge. Doniphan took on the Navajo and forced them to sign their first treaty of peace with the U.S. When Col. Sterling Price and his volunteers arrived from Missouri, Doniphan moved south to the Battle of Brazito and on to Chihuahua.

Price put down a rebellion at Taos, fought Indians and slowly brought a troubled peace to the new New Mexico Territory.

In the meantime, Lt. Col. Philip St. George Cooke forged a trained group of soldiers from Mormon immigrants and led the Mormon Batallion across southern New Mexico to California.

One of Kearny's soldiers. (Frost, 1851.)

Common soldiers were more informal in both dress and mounts. (Hughes, 1850.)

Col. Alexander Doniphan led troops south to Brazito and Chihuahua. (Hughes, 1850.)

Doniphan's troops marching through the Jornada del Muerto. (Richardson, 1848.)

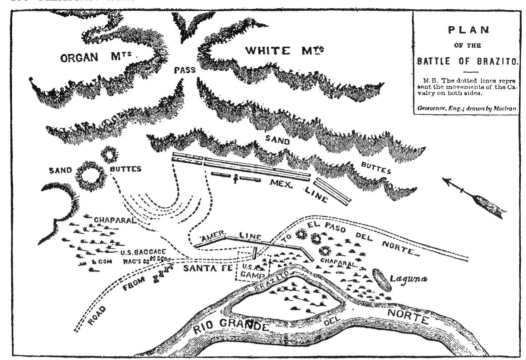

Battle of Brazito was the only battle of the Mexican War
fought in New Mexico. (Hughes, 1850.)

DONIPHAN's troops were camped at Brazito, nine miles
below Las Cruces, when 1,000 Mexican soldiers approached. Doniphan's 856 men prepared their long
rifles and, when the Mexicans were close, poured a
heavy and accurate rifle fire into them. The Mexicans
retreated, and many were killed by Apaches who had
been watching the battle from nearby hills.

Part of Doniphan's mule train. (Frost, 1851.)

Sterling Price, an officer with Doniphan, later became a
Confederate general. (Dunn, 1886.)

Kearny's troops crossing New Mexico mountains. (Harper's, July, 1880.)

Kearny's troops on their march through New Mexico. (All pictures on this page from Frost, 1882.)

Doniphan's men camped at the base of the Fra Cristobal Mountains. They marched on to meet Mexican troops at Brazito.

Capt. James Burgwin was killed during the storming of the Taos Church.

Doniphan's soldiers meet Mexican traders along the route south to Chihuahua.

Kearny's officers attend a baile at Santa Fe a few days after the town is taken.

Kearny's men camped at Valencia. The locals took advantage of army needs and charged 25¢ a stick for firewood.

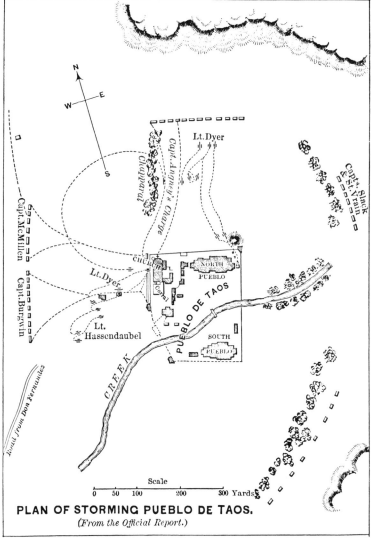

PLAN OF STORMING PUEBLO DE TAOS.
(From the Official Report.)

(Dunn, 1886.)

THE TAOS REVOLT started on January 19th, 1847. Townsmen and Indians killed Gov. Charles Bent, five other government officials, and nine Americans.

Col. Sterling Price and his Missouri Volunteers marched on Taos. They found most of the rebels barricaded inside the old mission at the pueblo. They bombarded it for two hours and returned the next day for a direct assault. Soldiers chopped holes in the walls and threw artillery shells inside.

At least 150 rebels were killed and the survivors surrendered the next day. Several of the leaders were executed and the revolt was over.

The Volunteer. Originally drawn to represent J. W. Patton immediately after first being under fire at Brazito. (Hughes, 1850.)

Doniphan's men met rancheros such as these while on the way to Mexico. (Hughes, 1850.)

Fort Fillmore in 1884. (*London Illus. News*, Dec. 2, 1854.)

Plan of Ft. Fillmore, sketched by Maj. James McKee, a surgeon at the post in 1861. (McKee, 1878.)

CIVIL WAR

FORT FILLMORE, built in 1852, was a small post along the Rio Grande near Mesilla. It was the first target of Col. John R. Baylor's troops in the beginning of the Civil War.

Baylor's men reached Mesilla late in July, 1861. On July 25th they confronted the Federal soldiers. After a short exchange of cannon balls and musketry the Union commanding officer, Col. Isaac Lynde, ordered a retreat to Fort Fillmore. The next day he ordered the fort abandoned.

The 800 Union soldiers were to surrender the fort to only 250 rebels. Lynde's officers were obedient but outraged.

The fort was abandoned and the soldiers trudged toward Fort Stanton. Baylor's troops, following behind, picked up stragglers by the dozens. Lynde surrendered his entire command to Baylor at St. Augustine Springs.

He was later dropped from the Army rolls amid charges of treason and cowardice.

Fort Cummings was built in 1863 on the Mesilla-Tucson stage road. (Bell, 1870.)

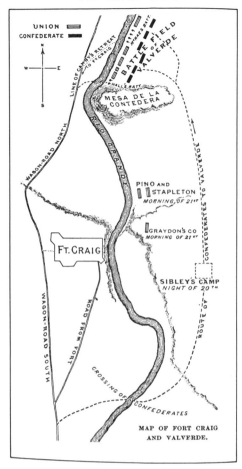

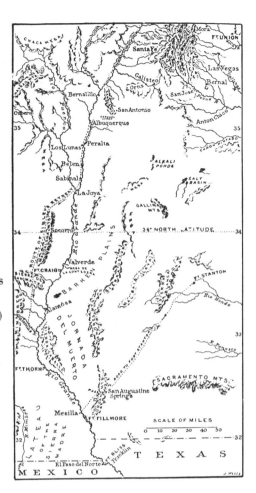

Overall map of Sibley's New Mexico Campaign. (Johnson, 1884.)

Map of Battle of Valverde. (Johnson, 1884.)

The ford on the Rio Grande near Fort Craig was the scene of the Battle of Valverde.   (Abert, 1847.)

Col. E. R. S. Canby was commander of the Union troops during the Civil War action in New Mexico. (Lossing, 1877.)

Gen. Henry H. Sibley headed Confederate Army in New Mexico. (Lossing, 1877.)

One of Sibley's "Texas Rangers," according to a Civil War historian. (Lossing, 1877.)

A more realistic view of one of Sibley's rangers. (Lossing, 1877.)

This first drawing of a Texas ranger appeared about a year before Sibley's invasion and was of one of Ben McCullough's Rangers in Richmond. The artist who made the later drawing (at left) probably copied directly from this woodcut, which explains the reversed sketch. (*Harper's Weekly*, July 6, 1861.)

Fort Thorn, near Hatch, was established in 1853 and abandoned in 1859. (Davis, 1857.)

FRONTIER FORTS

U.S. ARMY forts stretched along the Rio Grande to protect the Camino Real and across southern New Mexico to guard the Butterfield Trail. Fort Union took care of the Santa Fe Trail. Fort Bascom protected eastern New Mexico from the Comanches. Forts Stanton, Sumner, Lowell, Wingate, and Tularosa guarded Indian reservations.

The mountain men opened the west by trapping beavers for the beaver hats popular in the early 1800s. (*Century*, January, 1889.)

A scene along the Jornada del Muerto (Journey of Death) in southern New Mexico. (Richardson, 1867.)

When Fort Defiance was built in 1851, it was in a part of New Mexico that was later given to Arizona. Abandoned in 1861, it was reactivated in 1868 as a Navajo Indian Agency and still serves that function. (Dunn, 1886.)

"We closed at full gallop" was dime-novelist Mayne Reid's caption for this drawing. The reata looped above the Indian's head was actually used as a weapon during combat. (Reid, 1863.)

Navajo Indian (left) wearing a silver concho belt and other ornaments. The ornament resembling a crucifix was said to be a Navajo design for the morning star. (BAE *Report*, 1881.)

Fort Union lasted from 1851 to 1891. The fort itself never was the scene of any action, but it was an important personnel and supply depot for the military district of New Mexico. It is now a national monument. (Davis, 1857.)

The use of poisoned arrows by hostile Indians was a common myth. Hardly any of the North American tribes used poison, but unsanitary conditions often brought on blood poisoning in an arrow wound. The Indians of New Mexico did not, as shown here, use rattlesnake venom. (Tenney, 1880.)

Survivors of a forced march in winter reach Fort Massachusetts after a gruelling trip from Fort Bridger, Utah, in 1858. Capt. R. B. Marcy was in command. (Marcy, 1866.)

THE FRONTIER FORT was a prominent feature of New Mexico for fifty years. Except for Fort Marcy, built during the Mexican War, troops were at first stationed in rented barracks at such places as Rayado, Abiquiu, Cebolleta, and Socorro. After the first chain of forts had been built, locations were changed for reasons of health or convenience. Only a few of the forts were completely walled; most were clusters of buildings, usually adobe. A few temporary hay camps or other casual spots have been misnamed forts on some maps. Today the remains of some forts are being considered as possible sites for restoration.

Fort Massachusetts was established in 1852 in a strip of land that later became part of Colorado. This northernmost outpost in New Mexico was closed in 1858. (Peters, 1874.)

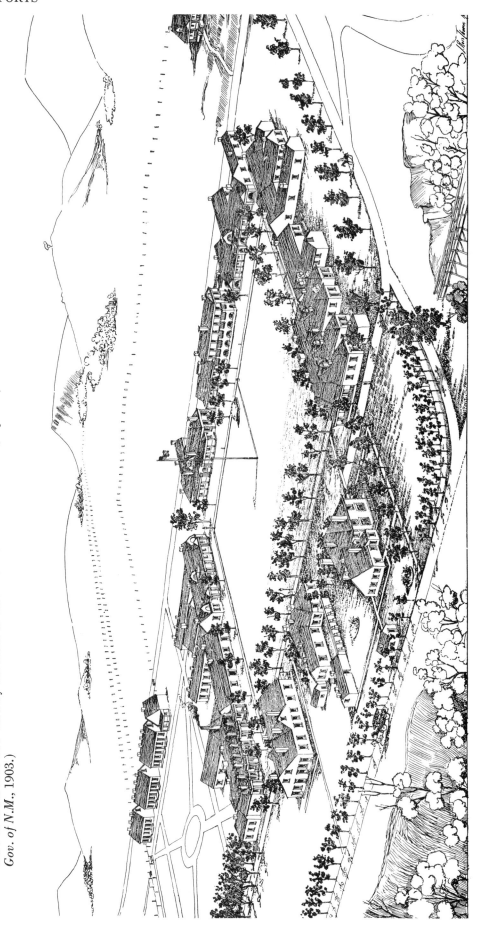

Fort Stanton as it was in the late 1800s. The fort was established in 1855 to protect the area from Apaches and, later, to control the nearby Mescalero Apache Indian Reservation. The buildings were partially burned during the Union retreat in 1862. The post was rebuilt and expanded. It was deactivated in 1896 and was a marine hospital from 1899 to 1953. It is now used by the State of New Mexico as a sanitarium. (*Report of Gov. of N.M.,* 1903.)

Dismounted cavalry drill, a new tactic, is tried by troopers at Fort Bayard. Soldiers sometimes used a breastworks of horses during a skirmish, but the horses had usually been killed in an ambush and not trained to lie down. This painting was made by one of the West's best-known artists, T. de Thulstrup, from a photograph made by pioneer photographer Christian Barthelmess. (*Harper's Weekly*, April 4, 1885.)

"The Apaches are coming!" A New Mexican Paul Revere spreads the news to isolated *ranchos* in this dramatic early drawing by Frederic Remington. (*Harper's Weekly*, Jan. 30, 1886.)

A cavalry trooper hoists the guidon to signal the main command during a scout after Apaches in the Arizona-New Mexico desert. (*Harper's Weekly*, July 17, 1886.)

The relaxed gentleman in the center is Nana, one of Geronimo's sub-chiefs. The engraver removed some wrinkles. Nana, by this time, was over eighty years old. The picture was taken in Mexico when he and Geronimo were preparing to surrender to Gen. George Crook. The engraving was made from several photographs taken by an enterprising photographer, Frank Randall, who accompanied Crook's expedition. (*Harper's Weekly*, April 17, 1886.)

Mescalero Apache leaders. Left to right, head chief San Juan, medicine man Gorgonio, and head war chief Nantzilli. (*Harper's Weekly*, May 29, 1886.)

GERONIMO!

GERONIMO, last leader of the "human tigers," hated Mexicans and Americans. He fought until 1886, when he surrendered for the last time and was sent to Florida.

He mellowed in later years and joined the Dutch Reformed Church.

Geronimo in captivity. (*Century*, May, 1889.)

Geronimo just before his surrender to Gen. Miles, from a photograph taken during an earlier conference with Gen. Crook. (*Harper's Weekly*, April 10, 1886.)

Charles McComas, son of Judge H. C. McComas. His kidnapping was the beginning of an Apache raid into New Mexico in 1883. Army troops followed the Apaches into Mexico until Geronimo surrendered. (*Harper's Weekly*, April 28, 1883.)

William Waldo holds off hostile Comanches and Kiowas during an attack on the Bent brothers trading party near Taos in 1829. (Triplett, 1885.)

Gen. George Crook commanded troops in Arizona from 1871-5 and from 1882-6. (*Harper's Weekly*, August 4, 1883.)

Officers' quarters at Fort Wingate. The fort was originally established at San Rafael, near Grants, in 1862 and moved to its present location in 1868. It was deactivated in 1911, but kept as a storage depot. (Beadle, 1873.)

APACHES had been raiding isolated ranches in New Mexico and Mexico for many years before they turned against the Americans in 1851. In that year, Mangas Colorado was flogged by miners at Pinos Altos and 35 years of war began. Mangas led raids in New Mexico until he was murdered in 1863 at Fort McLane.

Victorio, Loco, Cochise, Nana, and Geronimo continued the fight.

All sides, Army, Indian, civilian, and Mexican alike, indulged in massacres, ambushes, atrocities, and treachery during the Apache wars.

GENERAL CROOK's tactic was to use Apache scouts to help find and fight renegade Apaches.

"Flying columns" were organized by General Miles to pursue the hostiles relentlesly. His orders were, "Commanding officers are expected to continue a pursuit until capture."

Geronimo discussing peace terms with General Crook. (Kelsey, 1901.)

Army life in New Mexico was often lonely and dangerous. Courier duty, shown above, was more so than most other jobs. Stagecoaches, telegraphs, and heliographs carried many messages, but the courier was needed to carry messages and warnings between the isolated camps or forts and troops in the field. (*Harper's Weekly*, October 9, 1886.)

Geronimo is shown heliograph that could relay messages quickly across the desert. It was an important factor in ending the Apache Wars. (Miles, 1896.)

Apache mother and child. The child is on a cradle board that can be slung on the back. (*Century*, May, 1887.)

A common marker in the Southwest. (Cozzens, 1876.)

Apache braves in summer dress. (*Century*, May, 1887.)

Apaches scalping soldiers. This drawing is another that has been used many times. As originally published in *Harper's Weekly*, it showed Modocs scalping Gen. Canby in California. (Miles, 1896.)

CAPT. CRAWFORD.

The body of Capt. Emmett Crawford is brought to Lang's ranch near Cloverdale. When U.S. troops were chasing Geronimo in Mexico, Mexican soldiers thought Crawford's Apache scouts were hostiles and fired on them. Crawford stepped out to tell them to stop and was shot in the head by a Mexican scout. (*Harper's Weekly*, April 10, 1886.)

Apache scouts sent out to catch renegades sometimes brought back a head as proof of their efficiency. (Miles, 1896.)

Victorio, one of the greatest Apache war chiefs, was killed in an ambush in Mexico in 1880. (Ladd, 1891.)

Almost 300 Chiricahuas surrendered to Gen. Crook in 1886. Geronimo followed, saying "Once I moved about like the wind. Now I surrender to you and that is all." The next night, however, he got drunk and escaped with 40 followers. He remained hostile for another five months before surrendering to Gen. Miles. (Kelsey, 1901.)

A Comanche buffalo dance. The bison was important to
Comanche life, providing the tribe with food, clothing,
utensils, string, teepee covering and almost everything
else the Indians needed. They bartered the skins for cloth,
beads, and guns. (Eastman, 1874.)

Comanche on horseback, from an early
drawing. (Goodrich, 1849.)

Apache wickiups spread along the valley of the Mimbres
River. The domed huts were covered with brush or skins.
(Cozzens, 1876.)

Scout inspects deserted wickiup. (Whipple,
1853-4.)

Trouble near Fort Selden—a cowboy, insulted when an owner demanded a disputed steer be cut out of the herd, chases him off with a few bullets. (Powers, 1872.)

Comanches were a menace to travelers on the plains. Here they are preparing to attack a wagon train. (Cardona, 1892.)

Traveler Stephen Powers, who toured alone from coast to coast, is captured by Apaches near the New Mexico-Arizona border. (Powers, 1872.)

THE NAVAJO

THE NAVAJO TRIBE celebrated the 100th anniversary of its return to its homeland in 1968. Hundreds of Indians gathered at the Bosque Redondo and re-enacted the signing of the 1868 peace treaty and then made a symbolic march home. The Indians wore historic costumes and used traditional means of transportation while passing through the towns, but they rode a bus between cities.

Navajo braves in Santa Fe to discuss a truce with Comanches who were raiding the Bosque Redondo reservation. (Bell, 1870.)

Navajo in their best clothes make their way toward the agency for a head count and monthly rations. (Beadle, 1878.)

Before the American period, Navajo chiefs dressed more in the Spanish mode—were not quite as stylish as this picture by a French artist. (Domenech, 1862.)

FOR THE FIRST HALF of the 19th century, the Navajo roamed and raided as they had for hundreds of wears. In 1846, after New Mexico had been taken by Kearny's troops, Col. Alexander Doniphan marched out of Santa Fe with several hundred soldiers. His target was the Navajo tribe to the west. One column moved to the San Juan area and swept south. Another went up the Puerco River. Between them, they pinched a good part of the Navajo and collected them at Big Bear Springs, where Fort Wingate is today. There the Navajo signed the first of their treaties with the U.S. government.

The Navajo sweathouse is a primitive sauna. Water is poured over heated rocks; steam rises and fills the small, insulated hut. After an hour or two of sweating and singing, the Indians dash out and leap into a snowbank or stream. (B.A.E. *Report*, 1886-7.)

Navajo woman weaving a saddle blanket. The size of the loom determines the size of the finished work. Saddle blankets on this type of loom can be made with a minimum of work. Larger looms for rugs mean that the weaver must move around to pass the shuttle through the wool. (B.A.E. *Report*, 1882.)

The Navajo arrived in the Southwest about 500 years ago and began raiding the peaceful Pueblo Indians. The Apaches first appeared in Texas in the middle of the 16th century and were driven west into New Mexico by the Comanches.

This weaving scene of the 1870s would be the same on many parts of the Navajo reservation today. (*Harper's*, August, 1876.)

This drawing of a train was made by Choh, a young Navajo living near Fort Wingate. The sketch was made from memory and shows an unusually realistic style. (*Mag. of Am. Hist.*, Dec., 1889.)

Workshop of a Navajo silversmith. The Navajos learned the craft at the Bosque Redondo reservation near Fort Sumner. They began by counterfeiting metal ration discs issued by the army. They switched to silver work after they returned to their homelands. (Bur. of Eth. Report. 1890-1.)

Navajo shepherdess tends her flock in solitude on the reservation. (Brooks, 1887.)

Navajo woman (below) weaving a belt. (*Bur. of Eth. Report*, 1881-2.)

THE NAVAJO learned weaving from the Pueblo Indians in the 17th century. By the beginning of the 19th, they were the best weavers in the Southwest.

The same types of looms and spinning sticks have been used for 300 years.

The patterns used today were introduced by traders in the 1870s, and analine dyes supplied by them gradually replaced duller vegetable dyes. By 1890, the Navajo were selling all of their weaving.

William Army, the bearded one, led this group of Utes and Jicarilla Apaches and their agents on an exploration of the area between the San Juan and the Colorado rivers. (*Harper's Weekly*, Aug. 22, 1868.)

Kit Carson was born in Kentucky and came west at the age of 17 in 1826. He hunted and trapped from Chihuahua to Montana, drove sheep to California, and gained fame as John C. Fremont's guide on two expeditions. A colonel during the Civil War, he rounded up the Navajos in a winter campaign in 1863-4. He died in Fort Lyons, Colo., in 1868.

He was a small, sandy-haired modest man. When shown a dime novel with a picture of him holding a swooning woman and fighting off Indians, he stared at it for a long moment and said, "This here might have happened, but I ain't got no recollection of it."

Romanticized Carson was the basis for dime novels, TV shows and movies. (Above, Cozzens, 1876. Below, Beadle, 1878.)

Authentic sketch of Carson from a photograph. (Richardson, 1867.)

Carson in Union army uniform, from a photo. (Conard, 1891.)

Lt. Zebulon Pike led spying expedition into New Mexico. He was captured in Colorado in 1807 and brought to Mexico. His report helped start the Santa Fe trade. (Dunn, 1886.)

THEY LED THE WAY

Ceran St. Vrain partnered with the Bent brothers, brought Kit Carson west, lived in a lavish hacienda at Mora from 1860-90. (Conard, 1891.)

James P. Beckworth, a mulatto, trapped in New Mexico and later became chief of the Crows. (Beckworth, 1856.)

Richens Lacy "Uncle Dick" Wootton came to New Mexico in 1838, built 26 miles of toll road in Raton Pass in 1860. (Conard, 1891.)

Don Jesus G. Abreu, a Santa Fe boy, clerked in a Kentucky store, then moved to Missouri while he attended school on the savings he had garnered out of his wages of fifty cents a day. He returned to New Mexico and become a merchant at Rayado. (Haines, 1891.)

Solomon Luna was a prominent sheep owner. The Luna family once owned 150,000 head of sheep. Los Lunas is named for the family. (Haines, 1891.)

Col. J. Francisco Chaves, soldier, politician, attorney, educator, was murdered at Pinos Wells in 1904. (Haines, 1891.)

Rep. Stephen Elkins delayed statehood for New Mexico for 39 years by alienating Southern congressional votes. (*Leslie's*, Oct. 25, 1884.)

L. Bradford Prince came from New York in 1878 when he was appointed chief justice of the New Mexico supremè court. He served until 1882 and was appointed governor of the territory in 1889. (*Adobeland*, Aug. 1, 1891.)

Chief Narbona of the Navajo was killed by U.S. troops during a short fight while arranging a treaty between the two forces in 1849. (Simpson, 1850.)

Michael Cooney was the brother of James Cooney, who found gold in the Pinos Altos Mts. Michael took James' interests after he was killed by Apaches and became a leading figure in southwestern New Mexico. (Haines, 1891.)

Henry Lambert, a former chef for Presidents Lincoln and Grant, built the St. James Hotel in Cimarron in 1872. The hotel has had a lively history and is still in business. (Haines, 1891.)

Judge Warren Bristol came to New Mexico in 1872 from Minnesota to become a justice of the territorial supreme court. He presided at the trial of Billy the Kid in Mesilla. Bristol moved to Deming in 1885. (Haines, 1891.)

L. M. Keithley was the first Anglo settler in Las Vegas. He arrived there in 1839 and started a store and trading post. (Wilson, 1880.)

Lucien Maxwell owned the largest land grant in the world. It stretched from Springer to the Las Animas River, Elizabethtown to Raton—1,714,764 acres. (Conard, 1891.)

Nestor Armijo was born in Albuquerque and educated in St. Louis. He was a banker in Chihuahua, Mexico, until he escaped during the revolution of 1872 and moved to Las Cruces. (Haines, 1891.)

THE COMING OF COMMERCE

TRADE IN NEW MEXICO began in prehistoric times when Indians bartered at established centers like Taos Pueblo and the pueblo of Las Humanas that is now Gran Quivira.

New Mexico has always had relatively little industry and has depended heavily on trade and commerce. Supplies and goods traveled up the Camino Real to Santa Fe and along other primitive trails to other parts of the West. Heavy trading with the Midwest began in the 19th century when great wagons rumbled over the Santa Fe Trail. The traders fought bad weather, Indians, and dry-land pirates to bring their goods to Santa Fe.

Rich veins of gold were discovered at about the time of the Civil War, but nothing could be done with them because of the isolation of the areas and the danger of hostile Indians.

Then the Army moved in to protect the miners and settlers. Large cattle ranches started in the 1870s to supply the soldiers and a cycle of commerce began that is still going.

The railroads arrived to bring immigrants and settlers to take the open land, work the mines and swell the territory's population from 91,874 in 1870 to almost 200,000 by 1900. With the railroads came would-be cowboys, foreign remittance men, gamblers, tourists, tubuculars—just about every example of the human species.

New Mexico has always received much of its income from tourism and government spending.

The early reports on the area, from Cabeza de Vaca's to Zebulon Pike's, helped promote New Mexico. During the last half of the 19th century, many magazine articles, books, and government reports boosted the territory with tales of fertile land, rich gold strikes, buried treasure, fantastic scenery, a healthy climate, and the two subjects that have probably been most important to New Mexico tourism: cowboys and Indians.

Though many of the reports were fanciful, they brought the people who turned New Mexico into a thriving state.

The U.S. government, like the Spanish and Mexican ones, has had an important part in New Mexico's economy. The military arm, especially, has always had a big stake in the area since the days of matchlock muskets when careful soldiers waited patiently for a burning cord to ignite a flash pan of powder to fire their gun and hoped that the ball and powder hadn't fallen out of the barrel. Now New Mexico plays an important part in future flights into space.

Ore was crushed in stamp mills such as this. A drive wheel lifted the vertical hammer rods, letting them fall to pulverize the rock. The thunder of these old mills rumbled across the valleys, and the foundations of these mills still can be seen in abandoned workings (Bell, 1870.)

THE SPANISH conquistadores were disappointed in their search for gold, silver or quicksilver. Except for the copper mines at Santa Rita, there are few records of mining activity until gold was discovered in the Ortiz Mountains in the 1820s. Though hampered at first by crude mining methods and land grant problems, the mines blossomed in the late 1880s to produce millions in gold and silver.

Gold strikes were made in most of the mountainous areas of New Mexico. Mining camps sprang up in the Mogollons and the Black Range in the 1870s. The towns were plagued by Apaches, but they survived to produce more millions in gold.

Arrastra, powered by horse or burro, was used to grind ore under a heavy stone pulled around in a circular trough. (Drake, 1887.)

According to legend, Indian slave labor was used in the old Spanish mines of New Mexico. Actually, very little mining was done in those days. Simple ladders (right) made of notched logs were used in Indian pueblos and, later, in pit mines. (Ritch, 1885.)

Valley of the Santa Rita mines. (Bartlett, 1854.)

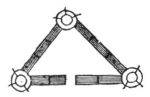

Plan of the presidio at Santa Rita. Fort Webster was later built near this spot. (Johnson, 1848.)

Triangular fort at the mines was built in 1803 by Francisco Manuel Elguea. (Bartlett, 1854.)

Stoping in a mine. This method is not used in a strip mine such as Santa Rita. (Thayer, 1888.)

FAMOUS MINES

COPPER was discovered at Santa Rita by Lt. Col. Manuel Carrisco in 1800. Mining started in 1803 and for 34 years the mule trains carried ore south to Mexico City for coinage at the royal mint. Lt. Zebulon Pike, taken on a tourist's journey in captivity through New Mexico, reported the mine was producing 20,000 mule team loads of copper each year.

Though the Apaches were not happy about having a copper mine deep in their territory, the area was relatively peaceful until 1837. In that year the State of Chihuahua put a bounty on Apaches. A warrior's scalp was worth $100, a squaw's $50 and the death of an Indian child was worth exactly $25 in gold pesos.

Two American entrepreneurs, Johnson and Gleason, took advantage of this business opportunity to stage a party at the dry lakes south of Santa Rita. They invited the local Apaches and their leader, Juan Jose. When the Indians had gathered around presents piled in the desert, a hidden howitzer loaded with slugs, nails, and chains was fired into their midst. When Johnson and Gleason and Mexican soldiers from the presidio at Santa Rita finished their business, some 400 Apaches were dead.

Juan Jose was one of the dead. Leadership of the tribe now fell on the shoulders of a vengeful firebrand called Mangas Colorado.

Under his guidance, the tribe cut off the supplies from Chihuahua to Santa Rita. When food ran short, the people of the town packed their belongings and moved south. Somewhere along the old trail to Chihuahua they were ambushed and slaughtered.

Greed and revenge had begun a blood bath in the Southwest that was to last for fifty years.

Panning gold in the mountains near Cerrillos. (Gregg, 1849.)

METHODS of mining vary. Panning or washing separates gold from sand by running water which washes away the sand and leaves the heavier gold. Panning is used to find gold in stream beds and also to help locate veins of it in bedrock along the stream.

With lode mining, ore is taken from tunnels and sent to a mill for processing. Crushed ore is treated with acid to dissolve the gold for later recovery.

Lode mining works veins of ore to be processed above ground. (Thayer, 1888.)

Lt. Emory's detachment, on reconnoissance, were among the first Anglos to pay an official visit to the Santa Rita mines. (Emory, 1848.)

NARROW GAUGE LINES

THE FIRST railroad entered New Mexico in 1879 after a dramatic stand by toll road owner Dick Wootton and engineer Ray Morley in Raton Pass. They and volunteers from Wootton's inn held off workmen of the Denver & Rio Grande line and saved the right of way for the Santa Fe line.

The Santa Fe went on to Las Vegas, Albuquerque, Socorro, and El Paso. Another lin branched off from Belen west to California. Another, now abandoned, went west from El Paso through the Hermanos and Peloncillo Mts. into Arizona.

The Santa Fe railroad uses switchbacks to climb Raton Pass. The pass is at an elevation of 7,834 feet. (Thayer, 1888.)

Toltec Tunnel (left) bores through the mountains along the Denver & Rio Grande narrow gauge railway near Chama. (Ritch, 1885.)

The "Chili Line" railroad in the 1880s went from Santa Fe, past Embudo (above), and into Colorado. (Ingersoll, 1889.)

Portal to the tunnel at Toltec Gorge on the Denver &
Rio Grande railroad in northern New Mexico. Efforts
are being made to preserve this narrow-gauge line.
(Ritch, 1882-83.)

The first railway train into New Mexico, from an old
sketch. The railroad doomed the Santa Fe Trail. (Inman, 1893.)

Lucien Maxwell's magnificent home at Cimarron was
always open to guests, including many noted travellers.
(Inman, 1893.)

Starvation Peak towers above the village of Tecolote near
Las Vegas. According to legend, about 120 Spanish colonists were besieged by Indians on the peak and starved
to death. Hermit's Peak, in the vicinity, is another landmark with a legend. (Higgins, 1896.)

An early cattle ranch in San Miguel county, owned by Mrs. S. B. Davis. (Ritch, 1885.)

OPEN RANGE DAYS

THE CATTLE business in New Mexico, as in the rest of the West, was once considered a get-rich-quick scheme. The idea was to lease, buy, or steal a piece of lush prairie, turn a few cows loose and let them breed into a fortune.

Things were not that easy.

Weather and diseases were highest on the list of pitfalls. A dry year, a snowstorm, or an epidemic could wipe out a ranch.

Rustlers were usually no menace, but occasional thieves, homesteaders, or cowboys would help themselves to a beef. The total was sometimes high.

Mismanagement and ignorance were other good reasons for going broke. Some ranches were owned by Easterners or foreigners who misplaced their trust in foremen and employees who had no loyalty to faceless bosses.

Overhead was also important. There were no rich cowboys, but a lot of hungry ones ate into the profits.

With all these drawbacks, fantastic profits still could be made by a rancher with good luck and experience.

New Mexico cattleman Charlie Siringo once estimated that a cow cost $4.75 to raise and $5.75 to get it to Chicago, where it could be sold for about $28.50—a profit of $18.

A cowboy trying to rope a steer this way, without dallying the lariat around his saddle horn, would lose either his rope or his arm. (Siringo, c1886.)

Any cowboy would be amazed to see such a neat, orderly column of cattle as drawn by this Easterner. (Siringo, c1886.)

Lambs in a corral on a ranch near Santa Fe. The sheep business in New Mexico is an old and respected one, with little of the friction with cattlemen that was seen in other parts of the West. (*Special Report*, 1892.)

Wool from one clipping on a New Mexico sheep ranch is shown ready for shipment. Profits on sheep could be high, but the business was plagued by the same troubles, including rustling, as the cattle business. (*Special Report*, 1892.)

PENITENTE BROTHERS

THE THIRD ORDER of St. Francis was founded in 1218 when painful penance was common.

It was introduced into New Mexico in 1598. Don Juan de Onate and his soldiers celebrated Holy Week with penance and scourging.

Though the custom died down in Europe, it continued in New Mexico. A group related to the Third Order became the Penitentes, or Brothers of Light. The Penitentes were sometimes the only religious organization in remote mountain villages that saw a priest only a few times a year.

In 1828, the new Mexican government expelled most Franciscan priests from Mexico and New Mexico. The Brothers of Light were left without leadership and sponsorship. They became an underground organization, unrecognized by the Catholic Church. While the Church ignored them, the Penitentes continued their old rites in a sort of open secrecy.

This scene (left) appears to be a masochistic frolic rather than a solemn religious rite. (*Harper's*, May, 1885.)

Night procession of hooded penitentes is led by the "pitero", whose shrill piping may be heard for miles in the high New Mexico mountains. (Darley, 1893.)

In the 19th century, Penitente ceremonies were more open and common than today. Early traders, usually Protestants, wrote scathing accounts of the Holy Week rites without mentioning or understanding the religious motives of the Brothers of Light.

Charles F. Lummis, in 1888, was the first to photograph the crucifixion. He did this with the protection of armed friends and later was almost murdered.

The Penitentes became more secretive toward the end of the 19th century. Few Anglos were invited to see ceremonies. Uninvited ones were turned away, sometimes beaten, sometimes killed.

Magazine writer Carl Taylor took pictures of Penitente ceremonies near Tijeras in 1936. Before he could mail off his pictures and story he was found shot to death in his lonely cabin. The pictures were gone.

A Penitente is crucified on Good Friday. Today he is bound to the cross on the local Calvary. In many villages in the last century he was actually nailed to the cross. (Darley, 1893.)

Many Anglos saw the Penitente rites including, shown above, Alex Darley, who wrote a lurid account of them. (Darley, 1893.)

The reata torture as depicted by Alex Darley. Methods of penance included scourging with cactus whips, cactus bound around the chest and head, and legs bound with cactus, raw-hide, or chains. (Darley, 1893.)

Procession of Penitentes at San Antonito, a small village in the Sandias. (Harper's Weekly, Sept. 7, 1889.)

Penitentes on their way to the local Calvary. (Darley, 1893.)

LEYES

para

EL GOBIERNO DEL TERRITORIO DE

NUEVO MEJICO.

LAWS

for

THE GOVERNMENT OF THE TERRITORY OF

NEW MEXICO.

—

TESTAMENTARIAS.

SECCION 1. Las leyes hasta ahora vigentes relativas á herencias, repartimientos, ultimas voluntades y testamentos segun estan contenidas en el tratado sobre estas materias escrito por Pedro Murillo de Lara, quedarán vigentes en todo lo que son conformes con la constitucion de los Estados Unidos y estatutos tambien vigentes

2 Los Prefectos concederán letras credenciales para testamenterias y para Abintestatos.

3 Las latras para testamentarias y Abintestatos serán concedidas en el condado en que el hogar ó lugar de residencia del difunto estubiere ubicado. Si no tenia hogar ó lugar de residencia al tiempo de su muerte y poseyera tierras las letras credenciales se concederán en el condado en ... s tierras ó parte de ... to no tenia hogar ó ... cia y no poseia tier ... drán concederse en ... m irió ó donde etu ... arte de sus bienes. Si

ADMINISTRATIONS.

Section 1. The laws *h*eretofore in force concerning descents, distributions, wills and testaments, as contained in the treatise on these subjects *w*itten by Pedro Murillo De Lorde, shall remain in force so far as *t*hey are in conformity *w*ith *t*he Constitution *o*f *t*he United States aud *t*he State laws in force for the time being.

2 The prefects shall grant letters testamentary and of administration

3 Letters testamentary and of administration shall be granted in the county in which the mansion house or place of abode of the deceased is situated. If he had no mansion house or place of abode at the time of his death, and be possessed of lands, letters shall be granted in the county in which the lands or a part thereof lies.

If the deceased had no mansion house or place of abode, and *w*as not possessed of lands, letters may be granted in the county in which he died or where the greater part of his.

CUADERNO

DE ORTOGRAFIA.

DEDICADO A LOS NIÑOS DE LOS SEÑO-

RES MARTINES DE TAOS.

Santa Fe 1834 *Imprenta de Ramon Abreu á Cargo de Jesus Maria Baca*

Page from the Kearny Code (above), the first book printed in New Mexico after U.S. occupation. Done in 1846, it was the initial code of laws for the new territory, with text in Spanish and English. Printing was done on the old hand-press brought by Josiah Gregg in 1834 and owned by Padre Martinez at the time of the invasion. (From original in Museum of New Mexico.)

BOOKS AND THE LAWS

The first book printed in New Mexico was a small spelling book, or *cuaderno de ortografia*, printed at Santa Fe late in 1834. Ramon Abreu owned the press at that time and Jesus Maria Baca was the printer. Padre Martinez wrote the little book, shown here in actual page size, and later owned the press. (Museum of New Mexico.)

THE BAD AND THE BRAVE

NEW MEXICO'S BEST KNOWN OUTLAW, Billy the Kid, overshadows the many others who visited or operated in the Territory.

Not that New Mexico was a paradise for outlaws. It was a crossroads, a sort of stopping place for the famous and infamous. Some stayed; others passed through on their way to safety or fame—as their own case may be.

Clay Allison was one of the West's deadliest killers. He liked to get drunk and ride the streets of Cimarron dressed in a gun belt, boots, and hat—nothing else.

Marino Leyba and his men robbed travelers in the San Pedros until the gang was captured, one by one, and taken to Albuquerque where they were quickly lynched.

Charles Kennedy kept an unusual inn high in the mountains near Elizabethtown in the early 1870s. Some of his more effluent customers didn't leave the place. Outraged citizens found human bones buried in his yard and hanged him, appropriately enough, in a slaughter house.

Many other well known Western lawmen or outlaws not generally associated with New Mexico spent time in the Territory. Doc Holliday had a dental office in Las Vegas while he dabbled in stage robbery and murder. Jesse James visited the town in its toughest days to see if there was room for him. He put up at the Montezuma Hotel and said he was a railroad man. He decided Las Vegas was too tough for him and moved on. Wyatt Earp had a profitable bunco game in Albuquerque's Old Town in 1882 until forced to move on.

Roy Bean lived in Mesilla before he was Law West of the Pecos. Bob Ford, killer of Jesse James, had a saloon in Las Vegas in 1889. Soapy Smith, king of the Yukon confidence men, learned many of his tricks in New Mexico. Buffalo Bill Cody owned a ranch near Cimarron.

Tom Horn was an Army scout in New Mexico before becoming a hired killer in Wyoming. Butch Cassidy and his Hole-in-the-Wall Gang hid out in New Mexico when things were too hot for them in Wyoming. Lou Blonger, Denver's crime king of the early 1900s, was a deputy marshal of Albuquerque in 1882. Burton C. Mossman, founder of the Arizona Rangers, grew up near Las Cruces and returned to the Pecos area to settle after travels in Arizona and Montana.

Bill Tilghman, Mysterious Dave Mather, Long Haired Jim Courtright, Bat Masterson, and even (so early biographies say) Wild Bill Hickock visited New Mexico.

But New Mexico was no haven for badmen. Justice was often fast and final, and if not swift enough by legal means, the citizens were willing to uncoil a rope.

Colorado bandit Charles Allison and his gang were captured by detective Frank Hyatt at a livery stable at 115 First St. in Albuquerque in 1881. Allison had specialized in stage and train robberies. He was sentenced to 37 years in the Colorado pen.

Filomeno Gallotti (below) and several others murdered four of his countrymen in Denver in 1875. He was tracked to Taos by detectives W. Frank Smith (left) and James Lewis, who grabbed Gallotti's gun hand to avoid trouble.

A local man named Thaw (right) had posed as a sheep buyer to lure Gallotti into the trap. (Both pictures from Cook, 1892.)

Slap Jack Bill (The Pride of the Panhandle) and Bull S. Jack were arrested for the robbery sketched below. They are shown being questioned by a U.S. Marshal in Santa Fe. (Hayes, 1880.)

NOTICE!
TO THIEVES, THUGS, FAKIRS AND BUNKO-STEERERS,
Among Whom Are
J. J. HARLIN, alias "OFF WHEELER;" SAW DUST CHARLIE, WM. HEDGES, BILLY THE KID, Billy Mullin, Little Jack, The Cuter, Pock-Marked Kid, and about Twenty Others:
If Found within the Limits of this City after TEN O'CLOCK P. M., this Night, you will be Invited to attend a GRAND NECK-TIE PARTY,
The Expense of which will be borne by
100 Substantial Citizens.
Las Vegas, March 24th. 1882.

FOR SOME SIX months, an infamous group of thieves, killers, and con men called the Dodge City Gang ruled the new town of East Las Vegas. Their leader was a dapper gent known as Hoodoo Brown. A justice of the peace, Brown held court in a saloon and rapped for attention with his Winchester.

The gang fled Las Vegas in March, 1880, after one of its members, policeman J. J. Webb, killed and robbed a rancher.

A warning poster was distributed by the Las Vegas vigilantes. Many copies of this poster, usually altered, have been printed. In some copies the date has been changed to 1881 because Billy the Kid was not alive in 1882. However, the Billy mentioned in this original was counterfeiter William Wilson. (Las Vegas, 1882.)

THE HOLDUP shown on the right happened in September, 1879, just a few miles out of Las Vegas. The stage to Santa Fe was stopped at Tecolote. The passengers filed out and were ordered to sit on a nearby log. Ex-Gov. William Arny had hidden his money. One of the bandits, possibly Doc Holliday, suggested that they search "the antedeluvian gentleman" again. The money was found on the second try.

Some of the hold-up men were members of the Dodge City Gang and the Las Vegas police force. Slap Jack Bill and Bull S. Jack were turned loose.

"Road Agents at Work" was drawn by Harper's artist W. A. Rogers, who was either an eyewitness or talked with the robbery victims the next day. (Hayes, 1880.)

A quarrel over cards at a New Mexico ranch as sketched by Frederic Remington. Time went slowly during winters on the ranches. There was little work and tempers were short. Scenes like this were common. (*Harper's Weekly*, April 23, 1887.)

Billy the Kid is killed by Sheriff Pat Garrett in Pete Maxwell's bedroom at Fort Sumner. (Garrett, 1882.)

BILLY, THE KID

Best known picture of Billy the Kid. (Garrett, 1882.)

Pat Garrett had a controversial life. He was murdered in 1908. (Garrett, 1882.)

Billy the Kid escaped from the Lincoln County jail in the courthouse on April 28, 1881. He shot one guard on the stairs, grabbed a shotgun and shot the second guard in the street. He found a horse, leaped into the saddle, fell off, jumped on again and rode off. (Garrett, 1882.)

Billy, Dave Rudabaugh, Billy Wilson, and Tom Pickett were captured on December 23, 1880, when they were hiding in a stone shack at Stinking Springs, near Ft. Sumner. Garrett and his posse killed Charlie Bowdre and cut off the fugitives' food supplies until they surrendered. (Garrett, 1882.)

Y DICIENDO ESTO LE HUNDIÓ EL PUÑAL EN MITAD DEL JADEANTE PECHO. PAG. 84.

Vicente Silva lured his wife to their ranch north of Las Vegas and stabbed her. (DeBaca, 1896.)

LA SOGA FUÉ ATADA Á UNA DE LAS BARANDAS DE HIERRO DEL PUENTE Y SU CUERPO LANZADO AL AIRE. PAG. 90.

Informer Patricio Maes was tried by the gang and hanged from a bridge. (De-Baca, 1896.)

¡ MUERE RUIN TRAIDOR MUERE ! PAG. 43.

Gabriel Sandoval, Silva's brother-in-law, was killed and buried in an abandoned cesspool. (DeBaca, 1896.)

THE FORTY BANDIDOS

VICENTE SILVA, saloonkeeper, operated in the Las Vegas area for about 15 years. He arrived in old Las Vegas in about 1875 and set up a saloon, the Imperial, that ran day and night.

He moved outside the law in about 1888. His gang, called the 40 Thieves, specialized in murder and rustling. By 1891 the town was ruled by thieves. In 1892, the owner of some stolen horses persuaded one of the gang, Patricio Maes, to show him where the horses had been hidden at one of Silva's ranches.

AL HABER VISTO AQUEL ESPECTÁCULO TAN HORROROSO SE ME CRISPARON LOS CABELLOS. PAG. 95

Cecilio Lucero murdered his cousin and a shepherd, tied the bodies behind two burros and let them remove the evidence. (Debaca, 1896.)

Vicente Silva. (DeBaca, 1896.)

JIRÓ EL ESCOTILLÓN CON RUIDO ESPANTOSO V CONMOVEDOR. PAG.112

Two of the 40 Thieves were hanged for murder. (DeBaca, 1896.)

SILVA was an outlaw after the discovery of the stolen horses. He sneaked back to Las Vegas to order the execution of the informer, Maes, and then killed his brother-in-law and wife.

After her burial, one of the members of the gang stepped up behind him, put his revolver behind the leader's ear and fired. Exit Silva.

SILVA CAYÓ AL SUELO COMO HERIDO POR EL RAYO, PARA NO LEVANTARSE MAS. PAG. '87.

The end of Silva—murdered by his own henchman. (DeBaca, 1896.)

TODOS CLAMABAN LA VENGANZA ! PAG. 96.

Cecilio Lucero was lynched for his crimes. (DeBaca, 1896.)

CON BASTANTE TRABAJO Y Á FUERZA DE PALANCAS É INGENIO LO PUSIERION EN UN CARRO PAG. 52.

The gang stole a safe from a Los Alamos store and found only $40 and postage stamps in it. (DeBaca, 1896.)

A HERITAGE PRESERVED

THE END OF THE NINETEENTH CENTURY saw rapid improvements in New Mexico's life and economy. The first telephones in New Mexico were used in Santa Fe in 1881. Graded, quality cattle replaced the wild longhorns. Cattle growers supplemented their stock with once-hated sheep. Albuquerque was lit by electricity in the 1890s.

The Twentieth Century brought more changes. New colleges began. Oil was discovered in Eddy County in 1909. Statehood came in 1912. Oil wells blossomed at Artesia and in the San Juan country in 1922. In 1945, almost a hundred years after Kearny's troops marched into New Mexico, the world boldly threw itself into the Atomic Age in one tremendous explosion near Alamogordo.

By this time the old torreons in the Manzano Mountain towns were gone. Drought and mismanagement had turned plains into deserts. Vandals and treasure hunters with picks, shovels, and sometimes dynamite had worked over ghost towns and forts.

Many of the old landmarks are gone. Huning Castle was torn down in 1955. Not even a modern supermarket or parking lot marks its site. One historic house in Santa Fe was razed in 1968 as part of an urban renewal program. The old Palace Hotel in Cerrillos was burned by vandals in 1968.

But there is some hope in preserving New Mexico's landmarks and heritage for the future.

The New Mexico Historic Sites Program is an ambitious project that will benefit the state and many of its communities. Some of the funds for the project will be provided by the federal government.

A state commission is determining which sites deserve priority in preservation or restoration. Fort Sumner, for instance, is to be an early project. Fort Cummings and the ghost towns of Mogollon and Shakespeare may also be sites for stabilization and identification for future visitors. In Santa Fe, the Barrio de Analco and several historic houses may be marked and preserved. The Plaza at Taos, Turley's mill, and several Taos County *torreons* may be protected. Some of the old trails may be included in the program.

Some day, visitors may see the old plazas of West Las Vegas and San Miguel del Vado, the towns of Mesilla and Santa Cruz, and areas like the Galisteo Basin in a state of historical preservation that will give people a picture of early New Mexico life without radically altering the economy and lives of the people who live in those places.

New Mexico's heritage has not been forgotten, and steps are being taken to keep it alive for the future.

SOURCES

ACKNOWLEDGMENTS

The pictures in this book came from nearly three hundred books, newspapers, or magazine articles. Many people suggested sources, found books, or gave access to rare items. These persons included David Otis Kelley, University Librarian, and Philip H. Fangman, Special Collections, University of New Mexico; Dr. John Polich, Mrs. Julia K. Shishkin, Mrs. J. R. Derryberry, and Nancy Gardetto, Museum of New Mexico; Jack D. Rittenhouse (who suggested and supervised this book), University of New Mexico Press; Dr. Myra Ellen Jenkins, New Mexico State Records Center and Archives; Mrs. Alys Freeze, Denver Public Library; Katherine McMahon, Albuquerque Public Library; Robert K. Dauner, University of New Mexico Photo Services; Phil Cooke, Press of the Territorian; Dale F. Giese; and Gil Campbell, U.S. Air Force Academy.

PICTURE SOURCES

Pictures have been reproduced from the source cited under each illustration, listed below in detail. Readers who wish to verify a fact in a caption will not necessarily find it in the same source as that of a picture.

Abert, Lt. James W. *Report of a Military Reconnoissance of the Arkansas, Rio Del Norte and Rio Gila,* Washington: 1847.

Adobeland. Albuquerque: 1881.

Adams, Eleanor. *The Missions of New Mexico, 1776.* Albuquerque: 1956.

Agriculture, U.S. Dept. of. *Special Report on the Sheep Industry.* Washington: 1892.

Bartlett, John R. *Personal Narrative of Explorations and Incidents in Texas, New Mexico, California, Sonora and Chihuahua.* London: 1854.

Beadle, John H. *The Undeveloped West . . .* Philadelphia: 1873.

————. *Western Wilds . . .* Cincinnati: 1881.

Beckwourth, James P. *My Life and Adventures.* New York: 1856.

Bell, William A. *New Tracks in North America.* London and New York: 1870.

Bourke, John. *Snake Dance of the Moquis.* London: 1884.

Brooks, Eldridge S. *The Story of the American Indian.* Boston: 1887.

Brown, William Horace. *The Glory Seekers.* Chicago: 1906.

Cady, Annie Cole. *The American Continent and its Inhabitants Before Columbus.* Philadelphia: 1893.

Cardona, Adalberto de, *De Mexico a Chicago y Nueva York.* Mexico: 1892.

Carruth, J. A. *Business Directory of Arizona and New Mexico.* Las Vegas: 1897.

Census, U.S. Bureau of. *Report on Indians Taxed and Indians Not Taxed.* Washington: 1890.

Century Magazine. New York: 1882-98.

Champney, Elizabeth W. *Great Grandmother's Girls in New Mexico.* Boston: 1888.

Chase, Charles M. *An Editor's Run in Colorado and New Mexico.* Montpelier, Vermont: 1882.

Conard, Howard L. *Uncle Dick Wootton.* Chicago: 1891.

Cook, David J. *Hands Up.* Denver: 1892.

Cozzens, Samuel W. *The Marvelous Country.* Boston: 1876.

Darley, Alex M. *The Passionists of the Southwest.* Pueblo, Colo.: 1893.

Daunt, Achilles. *With Pack and Rifle in the Far Southwest.* London: 1886.

Davis, W. W. H. *El Gringo.* New York: 1857.

De Baca, Manuel, *Vicente Silva,* Las Vegas: 1896.

Domenech, L'abbe Em. de. *Voyage Dans les Grands Deserts.* Paris: 1862.

Drake, Samuel Adams. *The Making of the Great West.* New York: 1887.

Dunn, J. P. Jr. *Massacres of the Mountains.* New York: 1886.

Eastman, Edwin. *Seven and Nine Years Among the Comanches and Apaches.* Jersey City, N.J.: c1873.

Ellis, Edward S. *History of Our Country.* Cincinnati: 1900.

Emory, W. H. *Notes on a Military Reconnoissance from Fort Leavenworth to San Diego.* Washington: 1848.

————. *Report on the U.S. and Mexican Boundary Survey.* Washington: 1859.

Ethnology, U.S. Bureau of. *Annual Report.* Washington: 1880-90.

Frost, John. *History of Mexico and its Wars.* New Orleans: 1882.

————. *Indian Wars of the United States.* Auburn, N.Y.: 1851.

————. *Thrilling Adventures Among the Indians.* Philadelphia: 1851.

Frost, Max. *New Mexico.* Santa Fe: 1894.

Garrett, Pat F. *Authentic Life of Billy the Kid.* Santa Fe: 1882.

Goodrich, Samuel G. *Manners, Customs and Antiquities of the Indians.* Boston: 1849.

Gregg, Josiah. *Commerce of the Prairies.* New York: 1849.

————. *Scenes and Incidents.* Philadelphia: 1856.

Haines, Helen. *History of New Mexico.* New York: 1891.

Harper's Magazine. New York: 1853-91.

Harper's Young People. New York: 1889-91.

Harper's Weekly. New York: 1861-96.

Hayes, A. A. *New Colorado and the Santa Fe Trail.* New York: 1880.

Higgins, C. A. *Guide to the Pacific Coast.* Chicago and New York: 1896.

Howe, Henry. *The Great West.* New York: 1852.

Hughes, John T. *Doniphan's Expedition.* Cincinnati: 1850.

Illustrated History of New Mexico. Chicago: 1895.

Ingersoll, Ernest. *The Crest of the Continent.* Chicago: 1889.

Inman, Col. Henry. *The Old Santa Fe Trail.* New York: 1897.

Ives, Lt. Joseph C. *Report Upon the Colorado River of the West*. Washington: 1861.

Johnson, R. V. and C. C. Buel, eds. *Battles and Leaders of the Civil War*. New York: 1887.

Johnston, Abraham. *Journal*. Washington: 1848.

Journal of American Ethnology and Archeology. Boston and New York: 1891.

Kelsey, D. M. *History of Our Wild West*. Chicago: 1901.

Ladd, Horatio. *The Story of New Mexico*. Boston: 1891.

Land of Sunshine. Los Angeles: 1894-8.

Las Vegas Hot Springs. Chicago: 1887.

Leslie's Illustrated Weekly. New York: 1877-94.

London Illustrated News. London: 1854.

Lossing, Benson J. *Pictorial Field Book of the Civil War in America*. Hartford: 1876-8.

Macomb, John H. *Report of the Exploring Expedition from Santa Fe, N.M. . . .* Washington: 1876.

Magazine of American History. 1889.

Marcy, Randolph B. *Thirty Years of Army Life on the Border*. New York: 1866.

Mayer, Brantz. *Mexico*. Hartford: 1852.

McKee, James C. *Narrative of the Surrender of . . . U.S. Forces at Fort Fillmore, N.M.* Prescott: 1878.

Miles, Nelson A. *Personal Recollections*. Chicago and New York: 1896.

Mills, T. B. *San Miguel County, Illustrated*. Las Vegas: 1885.

Mollhausen, Balduin. *Diary of a Journey from the Mississippi to the Coasts of the Pacific*. London: 1858.

Newberry, J. S. (See: Macomb.)

New Mexico, *Report of the Governor*. 1903.

Peters, DeWitt C. *Kit Carson's Life and Adventures*. Hartford: 1874.

————. *Life and Adventures of Kit Carson*. New York: 1858.

Popular Science. New York: 1874.

Powers, Stephen. *Afoot and Alone*. Hartford: 1872.

Reid, Mayne. *The Scalp Hunters*. New York: 1863.

Richardson, Albert. *Beyond the Mississippi*. Newark: 1867.

Richardson, William H. *Journal*. New York: 1848.

Ritch, William. *Official Report of the Territory of New Mexico*. Santa Fe: 1882-3.

————. *Aztlan*. Boston: 1885.

Roberts, Edward. *With the Invader*. San Francisco: 1885.

Sage, Rufus. *Scenes in the Rocky Mountains*. Philadelphia: 1854.

Santa Fe *New Mexican*. Santa Fe: 1881-2.

Schlagintweit, Robert von. *Die Santa Fe und Sudpacific-bahn in Nordamerika*. Cologne, Germany: 1884.

Schoolcraft, Henry R. *Information reporting the History, Condition and Prospects of the Indian Tribes of the U.S.* Philadelphia: 1856.

Scribner's Magazine. New York: 1891-3.

Simpson, James H. *Report*. Washington: 1850.

Siringo, Charles. *A Texas Cowboy*. Chicago: c1886.

Sitgreaves, Capt. Lorenzo. *Report of an Expedition Down the Zuni and Colorado Rivers*. Washington: 1854.

Speer, William S., ed. *Encyclopedia of the New West*. Marshall, Tex.: 1881.

Steele, James W. *Rand, McNally and Company's New Overland Guide to the Pacific Coast*. Chicago and New York: 1888.

Sweetser, M. F. *King's Handbook of the U.S.* Buffalo: 1891.

Taylor, Benjamin F. *Short Ravelings from a Long Yarn*. Chicago: 1847.

Tenney, E. P. *Colorado and Homes in the New West*. Boston: 1880.

Thayer, William. *Marvels of the New West*. Norwich, Conn.: 1888.

Triplett, Col. Frank. *Conquering the Wilderness*. New York and St. Louis: 1885.

U.S. Geographical and Geological Survey *Report*. Washington: 1881.

U.S. Govt. Doc., 1874: 43rd Cong., 1st Sess., H.R. Ex. Doc. No. 206, on private land claims.

Van Tramp, John C. *Life in the West*. Columbus, Ohio: 1867.

Wallace, Susan E. *The Land of the Pueblos*. Troy, N.Y.: 1889.

Whipple, Lt. A. W. *Report*. Washington: 1856.

Wilson, H. T. *Historical Sketch of Las Vegas*. (Chicago: 1880.)

Winsor, Justin. *Narative and Critical History of America*. Boston and New York: 1886.

Wood, Stanley. *Over the Range to the Golden Gate*. Chicago: 1889.

INDEX